Poetry Ireland Review 118

The Rising Generation

Eagarthóir / Editor
Vona Groarke

Poetry Ireland Ltd/Éigse Éireann Teo gratefully acknowledges the assistance of The Arts Council/An Chomhairle Ealaíon and The Arts Council of Northern Ireland.

LOTTERY FUNDED

Poetry Ireland invites individuals and commercial organizations to become Friends of Poetry Ireland. For more details, please contact:

Poetry Ireland Friends Scheme, Poetry Ireland, 32 Kildare St,
Dublin 2, Ireland

or telephone +353 1 6789815; e-mail management@poetryireland.ie

FRIENDS
Joan and Joe McBreen, Desmond Windle, Neville Keery,
Noel and Anne Monahan, Ruth Webster, Maurice Earls,
Mary Shine Thompson, Seán Coyle, Henry and Deirdre Comerford

Poetry Ireland Review is published three times a year by Poetry Ireland Ltd. The Editor enjoys complete autonomy in the choice of material published. The contents of this publication should not be taken to reflect either the views or the policy of the publishers.

ISBN: 1-902121-59-7
ISSN: 0332-2998

Assistant editors: Paul Lenehan and Sally Rooney, with the assistance
of Catherine Ward and Orla Higgins

Design: Alistair Keady (www.hexhibit.com)

Cover Credit: *25 cousins* by Lisa O'Donnell: oil on canvas, 165 x 200 cm
www.lisaodonnellartist.com

Contents

POETRY IRELAND REVIEW 118

Editorial

Make it new', decreed Ezra Pound with all the diffidence of Mrs Havisham instructing Pip and Estella to 'Play'. The truth is that neither novelty or playfulness is likely to respond positively to conditions created to encourage them: they are contrary gestures, and there's probably no surer way to stifle a creative impulse than to decide it must result in something new.

'New' is too big. It's like deciding to create something whole, or something pure: it can really only be recognised in hindsight. What is *newness*, anyway? 'Everything changes except the avant-garde', quoted Michael Donaghy (via Gore Vidal?) in a 1998 interview in *Metre*. Attempts to re-invigorate poetry through gestures of novelty tend to mothball pretty quickly, so that it never takes long for 'new' movements in poetry – flarf, the new concrete, L=A=N=G=U=A=G=E, post-internet poetry, and so on – to seem the equivalent of cribbage or quoits: all the rage for a minute or two (rarely even fifteen), but soon the preserve of the marginal eccentric, found only in virtual vintage shops and bought by no one with sense.

And yet, room has to be made for the new (whatever that is) if poetry is to exist outside of the cultural museum. There's new poetry all around us, in chapbooks, collections, at open mics and other readings, in magazines and online sites. You couldn't stanch the flow of it if you wanted to. It's new in the sense that it is freshly written, but also, perhaps, new in responding to poetic tradition in ways that have knowledge of contemporary life, and of the language we share to describe it.

This issue features thirty-six new poets. It seems strange to slap a defining number on newness, and I'm sure one reaction to this issue will focus on its omissions. Fair enough. But by the law of diminishing returns, it is possible to err on the side of inclusivity so far that the issue becomes prohibitively expensive to print and to distribute. Better this issue, with its inherent limitations, I think, than no issue at all. So, for better or worse (depending, I'll hazard, on whether or not you've been included in the issue), I set down parameters: to be eligible for consideration, you had to have published a pamphlet or a first collection in Irish or in English within the last five years. I know this necessarily excludes poets whose work I admire and which, I've no doubt, will go on to make a significant mark, and though I regret this, I also reckon that this probably won't be the last anthology of its kind, ever, and that other such opportunities will surely arise in the future.

I also acknowledge, as anthologists must, that in time this selection may look fusty or airy; that I may have gotten it all wrong, (there, I've said it), and that in twenty-five years, the poets who will have made a difference are not those featured here. It's possible, but I doubt it. I believe there's good and exciting work here, work that will continue to be honoured and enjoyed in all its many shades.

They're not all young poets (whatever that adjective might mean): I've always liked how poetry as an artform hooches up to make space for people who come to it late. It is the poems, as ever, I prefer to focus on.

So why then the questionnaire and its thirty-six sets of prose responses? Call it context. Or light entertainment. Or a new confessionalism. I thought it would help to show, alongside the poems, what kind of attitudes new poets strike when it comes to thinking about poetry and how it slips into or chafes against their otherwise lives.

It can be difficult to find an audience for your poems when you're starting out. Maybe especially nowadays, when there are so many busy words and bossy images to detain us on the way to the more subtle pleasures of a good poem. And finding an audience makes a difference. Solitude may well be a necessary poetic device, but it's probably not the most enjoyable human one. Which is why creative writing courses flourish, and writing groups and open mics and poetry readings too. Generosity is called for, I believe, and a nod of encouragement at the right moment can make a huge difference to a poet who feels she is speaking into the dark.

Poetry Ireland has been running its generous Introductions series of readings by new poets for many years now. It's heartening to see so many new poets here who have found an initial forum there. Something's going right when the mechanisms in place for encouragement actually result in the writing of poems. Good poems too; poems with vigour and grace and bravura and flair. I've greatly enjoyed editing this issue, encountering poems that have very little in common other than a commitment to the art of writing poems. Thirty-six poets: a wide enough choice for a huge range of subject matter and approaches. Wide enough, I hope, to illustrate how vibrant poetry is in Ireland, how far from being jaded or defeatist, how it likes to throw shapes and fool around, but also to insist how crucial poetry remains.

Thank you to all thirty-six poets featured here, for their complicity, enthusiasm and very good poems. And thanks to Sally Rooney and Paul Lenehan for pulling the thing together like so many instruments making, between them and the poets, what I hope is some kind of gorgeous, new sound.

– Vona Groarke

30 Questions for The Rising Generation

Each of this issue's contributors was invited to answer some or all of the following thirty questions, within a maximum of three pages.

Were you a strange child with a taste for verse?

Do you too dislike it?

Who is your favourite character in a poem?

If you could die and come back as a poem, what poem would it be?

Someone offers you €1,000,000 to never write again: what is your response?

Have you ever glued pages of a poetry book together?

It's the centenary of the Easter Rising: does this fact matter to you and if so, in what way?

If someone described you as a political poet, what would your reaction be?

Would you rather be the poet or the poem?

If you could pick a time to be dropped amongst the three best poets alive at that moment, when would it be and who would they be?

What's your worst poetry habit?

You've arranged a date for 8pm, but it's 8.10pm now. You're working on a poem and it's going well. What do you do?

Have you ever carried a poem by someone else around on your person?

A family member says, 'You should write a poem about that': what do you do?

If your best poem were a weekend away, where would it be?

It's a good poem but it's forty-one lines long and the competition with the big prize specifies a max of forty: what do you do?

Have you ever used a poem to seduce someone? If so, what poem was it? (And did it work?)

You're given a choice: either every poem or no poem you write from now on must use the word 'I'. Which do you choose?

Your friend is depressed: what's the very last poetry book you'd give him/her?

Who will play the poet in the Hollywood adaptation of your last poem?

You're invited to read in a major festival: what are your top three back-stage demands?

What's your current favourite word?

You're proud of the poem but know it will offend someone you don't even like: what do you do?

Would you rather win the TS Eliot Prize or the Prize Bonds?

Let's assume you're 60 and still publishing poems: what do you want to have achieved between now and then?

Cyril Connolly said the true function of a writer is to write a masterpiece and no other task is of any consequence. Do you agree?

'The hard part is getting to the top of page 1' – Tom Stoppard. What, for you, is the hardest part of writing?

If your ideal poem were an outfit, what would it look like?

What advice would you give older poets?

Is there any question you wish you'd been asked here (that you'd like to answer now?)

Graham Allen

SYDNEY PARK, SPRING 2015

We are coming to the end of winter.
Folds of steam are swagging up

from the river-hugging, splintered town.
The sun is returning.

Light is welling, spreading
itself like water fills a tank.

Along the footpath and the walled house gardens
a thousand things I have no words for

are being born.
I am no field botanist, gauging

the heliotropic scene.
I am not Adam in Paradise

confronted with the nameless beasts.
I am a survivor of the unspecified worst,

surprised by my own persistence,
shocked by contingency,

the last guy standing as the credits come down
at the end of an old disaster movie.

If not from scratch, then still, somehow,
we are going to have to start over again.

Graham Allen

NOT YOU

Tonight there is defeat.
The moon is absent.
Nothing fits.

Across the landing
people you will never know
are screaming at each other.

The radio news counts numbers
of unemployed,
the t.v. is full of junk.

The novel you selected
and positioned on the table
is too painful to commence.

You have not met your daughter
for six whole months.
Nobody calls.

The notebook you bought last week
is empty,
save for five aborted lines.

The internet is down,
your limbs creak,
your lips are cracked, lacking balm.

That photograph of yourself
hours before graduation
is no longer representative.

You have forgotten everything
you ever knew about the fossils
arranged on the mantelpiece.

Outside the house, beyond
the constant traffic, someone,
not you, is looking at the stars.

Graham Allen

Were you a strange child with a taste for verse? In my childhood there was
the Bible and the Salvation Army Songbook. I was particularly drawn to
the 'Heaven and Hell' and 'Death and Judgement' sections of the latter,
especially the idea of eternal damnation committed to verse.

Do you too dislike it? What?

Who is your favourite character in a poem? Toss of a coin between PB Shelley's
Demogorgon and Tennyson's Ulysses.

If you could die and come back as a poem, what poem would it be? Tennyson's
'Tithonus', but somewhat revised on the eternal youth issue.

Someone offers you €1,000,000 to never write again: What is your response? Go
away!

Have you ever glued pages of a poetry book together? Why would anyone do
that?

*It's the centenary of the Easter Rising: does this fact matter to you and if so, in
what way?* It matters to everyone a great deal. It matters that this particularly
important milestone in the young history of this nation is not reduced to
a media fest in which nostalgia is dished up to pander to prevailing
conservative rule. Heroes and martyrs gave their lives to establish a
Republic in which all people would be respected. Currently this nation is
being held captive by a cabal of career politicians, bankers, bond-holders
and members of the establishment. Time to remember why people gave
their lives. Time to make Ireland the kind of beacon for freedom it was
meant to be.

If someone described you as a political poet, what would your reaction be? Of
course I am! Is there something wrong with political poetry?

Would you rather be the poet or the poem? A poem depends on the existence
of a poet. If I chose to be a poem I would be choosing to be the creation
of someone else. Who chooses that?

*If you could pick a time to be dropped amongst the three best poets alive at that
moment, when would it be and who would they be?* I've spent my academic
life thinking about and reading the Romantics (my three in particular
PB Shelley, Mary Shelley and Blake – add Byron and Wordsworth if you
will), so it would have to be the turn of the nineteenth century.

What's your worst poetry habit? I am a vinyl record. I tend to get stuck in a groove. I have to slap the record player hard to make the needle jump back into the flow of the music. Could be I need to replace the needle. Could be all my favourite LPs are scratched.

You've arranged a date for 8pm, but it's 8.10pm now. You're working on a poem and it's going well. What do you do? Text ahead. We have these wonderfully convenient machines nowadays!

Have you ever carried a poem by someone else around on your person? If so, what was it? Do you not have poetry by others on your person?

A family member says, 'You should write a poem about that': what do you do? I smile and try not to yawn.

If your best poem were a weekend away, where would it be? On the banks of Lake Trasimeno in Umbria.

It's a good poem but it's forty-one lines long and the competition with the big prize specifies a max of forty: what do you do? If I think it has a chance I look to see if alterations can be made without harming the poem. If they can't then the big prize is a loser.

Have you ever used a poem to seduce someone? If so, what poem was it? (And did it work?) I find that poetry is heightened by the experiences of desire and love. I don't know about seduction, which sounds a bit calculating. I have definitely written about sexual desire and about completely losing touch with someone you used to touch. As far as this subject is concerned, poems are messages folded inside small bottles cast adrift in the ocean.

You're given a choice: either every poem or no poem you write from now on must use the word 'I'. Which do you choose? cf. Coleridge's *Biographia Literaria*, Chapter 13. According to that famous piece of literary theory there is really no choice in the matter. In my **HolesbyGrahamAllen.org** I try to exploit the potentiality in general and indefinite pronouns.

Your friend is depressed: what's the very last poetry book you'd give him/her? I think I might hide my recently acquired copy of Geoffrey Hill's *Broken Hierarchies*.

Who will play the poet in the Hollywood adaptation of your last poem? Steve Carrell.

You're invited to read in a major festival: what are your top three backstage demands? An end to Western political interventionism. The eradication of religious indoctrination from all educational syllabi. The appointment of Malala Yousafzai to Secretary General of the United Nations.

What's your current favourite word? Annihilate.

You're proud of the poem but know it will offend someone you don't even like: what do you do? Publish with a smile.

Would you rather win the TS Eliot Prize or the Prize Bonds? How much am I winning if the latter?

Let's assume you're 60 and still publishing poems: what do you want to have achieved between now and then? You do realise that's only eight years away for me! I hope to have published two or three more collections, to have established **HolesbyGrahamAllen.org** as one of the leading examples of e-poetry, and to have written something with which I can truly be happy.

Cyril Connolly said the true function of a writer is to write a masterpiece, and no other task is of any consequence. Do you agree? No I do not. That might be the most important personal and aesthetic goal, but I would rather stay with Shelley's notion of the social function of poetry as a window towards a possible future. That window opens in lots of different ways.

'The hard part is getting to the top of page 1' – Tom Stoppard. What, for you, is the hard part? Being satisfied.

If your ideal poem were an outfit, what would it look like? An as-yet-unseen Bowie costume from the late 1970s.

What advice would you give to older poets? I am neither a young man nor an 'old poet', so I simply say to one and all: if you're not trying to swerve away from what has already been written you're not trying hard enough to earn the title of 'poet'. Those who are swerving decisively don't need my advice.

Is there any question you wish you'd been asked here (that you'd like to answer now?) Would you like to name your fee?

Tara Bergin

NOTES FROM THE SANATORIUM

It would have been better to cross with the nuns –
like A—— did in Rome –
like P—— did that time he was far from home –
to wait, and cross with them anonymously!
I have always had far too much of myself in me.
In my heart. In my chest.
And even though it's not actually late –
not in the real world –
it feels late.
But who wants to listen?
Not me.

You see it's not a safe road
but at the same time it's not daring.
At times I fear the link is broken, or breaking.
At times I fear all my letters are lost.

Frugal living has a high cost.

I don't talk to my lover, or to my friend who has emigrated.
I don't talk to my brother, or to my friends – not since I emigrated.
I only talk to faces I don't know,
and their thoughts don't always show.

I longed to be a —— of great renown,
but I can see that I needed to sell it better.
It's all I can do, and yet, lately, I feel I can't –
the sick eye, the sick ear.
My limitations are: I have no foresight.
I cannot hear.
Not the subtle noises.

And this is how it feels.

If everything we wanted was the same,
if everything we wanted was right,
how could anyone be renegades?
How could we really know the night?

After times like these,
I want to fall on my knees.
After talking like this,
I blush to the roots of my hair.
To the roots of my soul,
the soul I pass around everywhere.

ANSWER TO A QUESTIONNAIRE

From the fat, tight fists of babies
I steal ideas; I steal similes;
and these I exchange for butter
and for bread.

For example, yesterday I said:
today we have the strange-sounding call
of a short-eared owl.
I said it to the baby.
This is the task for today, I said,
and I pleaded that the baby give me something.

The baby listened to the shriek of the owl.

Please, I said, or I will have nothing –
I will be bereft – this will affect you too.

The baby was a good little baby.
It opened its plump little fist,
and I stole from it:
goodies, high-pitched.
This morning, I pawned it all
for some butter and some bread.

That's just one example.

Tara Bergin

Were you a strange child with a taste for verse? As a young child I did plenty of reading and writing but I wasn't what you would call sophisticated in either. It was just normal life. As I grew up, and the real world started to interfere, it became more obvious that these things weren't accepted as normal, and that they needed to be protected. As a teenager I would bunk off school, but I just spent the time working on my English home-work, which was the only school work I enjoyed. I didn't do well at school. Formal education began for me much later, as a mature student. This was my second chance, and it was really only then that I developed what you might call a 'taste for verse', in the sense that I could start to understand what the Modernists were up to.

Do you too dislike it? The reason I know that this question refers to the first line in Marianne Moore's poem, 'Poetry', is that it was quoted to me several years ago, as advice for my own writing – that irritating line about imaginary gardens and real toads. I was advised – quite correctly – that the poem I'd submitted for comments needed more 'real toads'. I've never quite been able to like this poem after that.

Who is your favourite character in a poem? The old guy who enters just at the end of William Carlos Williams' poem 'Death the Barber' saying 'Sunshine today!' I think this is a perfect poem in many ways. I read it regularly, and always with total pleasure at how it works.

If you could die and come back as a poem, what poem would it be? Patrick Kavanagh's 'On Raglan Road', as long as I could come out of Luke Kelly's mouth.

Someone offers you €1,000,000 to never write again: What is your response? No hesitation.

Have you ever glued pages of a poetry book together? I've glued pictures on top of the covers of one or two.

It's the centenary of the Easter Rising: does this fact matter to you and if so, in what way? As an Irish woman I am keenly aware of independence. I am suspicious of any systems of power or of being told how to behave. As a poet, I am also aware of the need to be outside of experience, in order to write about it. But perhaps most pertinently, I am aware that homesick-ness can stir up dangerous emotions – a certain rose-tinted sentimentality that must be treated with extreme caution. As an Irish poet living and working in England, I miss home – which suggests that I am the last person to be trusted with a question such as this.

If someone described you as a political poet, what would your reaction be? As an egotist: tell me more.

Would you rather be the poet or the poem? If we're talking about one of my poems, most certainly the poet. My characters inhabit strange and disturbing worlds.

If you could pick a time to be dropped amongst the three best poets alive at that moment, when would it be and who would they be? In the summer of 1972 Ted Hughes, Seamus Heaney and the Hungarian post-Holocaust poet János Pilinszky met for dinner in London to discuss the English translation of Pilinszky's poems. I'd pull up a chair to that table.

What's your worst poetry habit? Lack of habit. I wish I had more of a routine.

You've arranged a date for 8pm, but it's 8.10pm now. You're working on a poem and it's going well. What do you do? Rejoice: it's the best possible outcome.

Have you ever carried a poem by someone else around on your person? If so, what was it? I always carry poems, or bits of poems, around. They are like touchstones in a world where nearly everything else makes me feel like a foreigner. At the moment I've got a copy of 'Bobby Shafto' tucked in my pocket. It occurred to me that this English nursery rhyme is strangely similar to the traditional Irish song 'Dónal Óg'. In both, the beautiful fair-haired boy goes off to sea, promising to come back and marry the girl. But I don't think Bonny Bobby Shafto is ever coming back.

A family member says, 'You should write a poem about that': what do you do? Listen very carefully and wonder what it says about the way they see my poems. I told you I was an egotist.

If your best poem were a weekend away, where would it be? Streedagh in a heat wave. Rare.

It's a good poem but it's forty-one lines long and the competition with the big prize specifies a max of forty: what do you do? Rejoice: it's the best possible outcome.

Have you ever used a poem to seduce someone? If so, what poem was it? (And did it work?) I once sent a book of poems to someone I met briefly at an art exhibition. It worked. Not only are we married now, but I get to read the book whenever I want.

You're given a choice: either every poem or no poem you write from now on must use the word 'I'. Which do you choose? Weirdly enough, the other day the letter 'i' on my computer keyboard got stuck. I fixed it by using a child's tiny paintbrush to brush away some biscuit crumbs. But I took it as a sign – not to stop eating biscuits near my computer, but to be more objective in my poems.

Your friend is depressed: what's the very last poetry book you'd give him/her? Poems to Read at Your Wedding.

Who will play the poet in the Hollywood adaptation of your last poem? Harry Houdini.

You're invited to read in a major festival: what are your top three backstage demands? There's a backstage?

What's your current favourite word? Remorse. Literally, it means 'the gnawing pain of conscience'.

You're proud of the poem but know it will offend someone you don't even like: what do you do? Publish it. Feel horrified. Comfort yourself with the thought that no one will read it. Feel horrified.

Would you rather win the TS Eliot Prize or the Prize Bonds? Easy.

Let's assume you're 60 and still publishing poems: what do you want to have achieved between now and then? Self-knowledge.

Cyril Connolly said the true function of a writer is to write a masterpiece, and no other task is of any consequence. Do you agree? For poets, it doesn't quite make sense. Eliot's advice is better: 'Those who expect that any good poet should proceed by turning out a series of masterpieces … are simply ignorant of the conditions under which the poet must work … The poet's progress is dual. There is the gradual accumulation of experience … it may be only once in five or ten years that experience accumulates to form a new whole and finds its appropriate expression.' I agree with that.

'The hard part is getting to the top of page 1' – Tom Stoppard. What, for you, is the hard part? Getting beyond page one. The longer I work on something, the shorter it gets.

If your ideal poem were an outfit, what would it look like? Joseph Beuys' Felt Suit.

What advice would you give to older poets? Don't hate your most popular early poems. Read them to us, once in a while.

Dylan Brennan

CHRISTMAS, OAXACA

Noche de rábanos. A giant flea nursing a bottle of mezcal, a bug-eyed parrot swaying in the evening breeze, a pastoral tableau, an abundance of nativity scenes. We duck in through a gap in the railings to get to the interior where something vile awaits us amid the posters and the placards – his perfect teeth surrounded by this crimson mess of exposed flesh. We didn't ask to see this and we move away, drifting the choppy rivers of brass bands that march down the streets, each trying to drown the other. Trucks with children dressed as angels and shepherds followed by dancing girls with magnificent layered skirts and men holding bamboo-framed giants with papier mâché heads. All dance and twirl, multi-coloured dervishes enraptured in their shared dreams. Earlier I'd seen a boy play a sousaphone he'd fashioned from plastic water bottles, begging for cash. I look for him now but, of course, he doesn't feature. This event is important – these instruments impeccable. Metallic and polished they twinkle in the night. Fireworks exploding and a rain of sulphur and primary colours bathes us all in its pungent glow. Children everywhere, pregnant girls everywhere and the blank stares of the *normalistas* in the background – all is magnified, all there is to be gobbled up like fried grasshoppers, life and death in every blink. Prawn bisque with roasted almonds, piping hot turkey with a fruits-of-the-forest sauce, stuffing infused with apricot purée, pears soaked in aniseed and red wine with cinnamon ice-cream. The noise of the fireworks and the parading *mojigangas* diminishes slowly while we eat. After coffee a little girl plays an accordion on the corner and I give her some coins. Back to bed through the *zócalo*, a shrine of purple candles and lights in the shape of 43. A text message from the local news service tells us Peña Nieto, the charm president, the hair-cut president, wishes all a happy Christmas, a peaceful Christmas and an end to violence. A poster picture of that boy with a young lady and a baby in his arms and I wonder if, in their dreams and memories, that smile will return to them or if they'll be faced with an abomination, red and despicable and on the shores of obsidian sleep I wonder what they did with his eyes and I close my eyes.

Dylan Brennan

THINGS YOU CAN DO WITH A GRASSHOPPER (OR: OF GRASSHOPPERS
WHICH SING THE BETTER WHEN THEIR HEADS ARE CUT OFF, AND
REVIVE SPONTANEOUSLY AFTER BEING LONG DEAD)

If you decapitate a grasshopper it will sing
for you sweetly for a while before dying.

Like a religious martyr or a narco rat –
of more consequence in death than in life.

If you place a grasshopper up to his neck
in the snow he'll stay congealed for a time

until you return to find him and decapitate
him then (the dulcet tones all the more delicious

for having waited a full season for that insect
harmony). Or, by the warmth of your hands

and breath, you could coax one back to wonder.
You could pluck a whole batch from fields

of trampled ice and, when you feel the hop
and flutter of rebirth tickle your fingers,

release them in the meadows of a land
where we've not yet begun to behead.

Dylan Brennan

Were you a strange child with a taste for verse? All children are strange aren't they? I used to carry around a tiny blue hardback copy of *Shakespeare's Sonnets* in the buggy when I was two years old. Not reading it, obviously, but just carrying it around. So I must have liked the feel of a book before anything else. But I remember, when I started primary school my first love was joke books. I'd take them home from the library and memorise them. Why did the robber take a bath? To make a clean getaway. A love for silly puns surely led me to poetry.

Do you too dislike it? No.

Who is your favourite character in a poem? Has to be Prufrock. Reading 'The Love Song' for the Leaving Cert was a big moment for me, like *The Catcher in the Rye*. And I have my father to thank for both; he was my English teacher for a couple of years. I still remember misquoting Eliot in the mock exam. Instead of 'I should have been a pair of ragged claws/ Scuttling across the floors of silent seas', I wrote 'I wish I was a crab.' I think (hope) that was just to wind up the old man. Either way it worked.

If you could die and come back as a poem, what poem would it be? 'The Frost' by Michael Longley, or that one about Venus bringing everyone back home by Sappho. Anything by Nezahualcóyotl.

Someone offers you €1,000,000 to never write again: What is your response? Take the money; keep writing.

Have you ever glued pages of a poetry book together? No. Not poetry.

It's the centenary of the Easter Rising: does this fact matter to you and if so, in what way? Yes, it does. Look at the Labour Party now. Remember how we started banning books after independence. How we handed over control of education to the church, how we started murdering each other over a treaty. Though simplified by the state as a heroic act, the Rising is intriguing – one big complex clusterfuck that we still haven't gotten our heads around. Still a lot to be learned.

If someone described you as a political poet, what would your reaction be? It has happened and I don't care. A poet can write about whatever s/he wants and that, in itself, is political.

Would you rather be the poet or the poem? I wish I was a crab.

If you could pick a time to be dropped amongst the three best poets alive at that moment, when would it be and who would they be? I'd like to be dropped into Tarahumara peyote territory with Antonin Artaud around 1936 and accompany him on his mad journey to Ireland, in a quest to return St Patrick's staff to the Irish people. Then we could knock into Kavanagh's place for a cup of tea.

What's your worst poetry habit? Hoping someone will read what I write.

You've arranged a date for 8pm, but it's 8.10pm now. You're working on a poem and it's going well. What do you do? This question is giving me flashbacks of the Department of Foreign Affairs 3rd Secretary exam. I think all the answers were supposed to be 'take no initiative, ask a superior, pray for guidance'. Obviously this all depends on who's waiting for me but I'd probably just finish the poem on the bus or in my head, depending on how the date's going.

Have you ever carried a poem by someone else around on your person? If so, what was it? I used to carry short Ungaretti poems around in my wallet on scraps of paper. They sometimes came in handy (see below).

A family member says, 'You should write a poem about that': what do you do? Leave the room.

If your best poem were a weekend away, where would it be? Dublin in spring, Pyongyang in summer, Venice in autumn and Christmas in Oaxaca.

It's a good poem but it's forty-one lines long and the competition with the big prize specifies a max of forty: what do you do? Leave it alone. Good poems don't always win prizes. Don't enter, no bloodlust when you read the winning poem.

Have you ever used a poem to seduce someone? If so, what poem was it? (And did it work?) Yes. 'Sentimento del tempo' by Ungaretti. Yes, it worked. 'Into My Arms' by Nick Cave has also served me well over the years.

Your friend is depressed: what's the very last poetry book you'd give him/her? James Franco's *Directing Herbert White*.

Who will play the poet in the Hollywood adaptation of your last poem? Seeing as Rod Hull is no longer with us, James Franco. Though my students tell me I look like Zach Galifianakis (the fat guy with the beard from *The Hangover*) and 'Adele's boyfriend'.

You're invited to read in a major festival: what are your top three backstage demands? I'll never make any backstage *demands*. However, a bottle of wine and a bathroom would be nice. And a corkscrew.

What's your current favourite word? Popocatépetl. It's a volcano outside Mexico City. The word means 'smoking mountain' and I can see it on my way to work, smouldering on the horizon, ready.

You're proud of the poem but know it will offend someone you don't even like: what do you do? Publish it.

Would you rather win the TS Eliot Prize or the Prize Bonds? TS Eliot I suppose. At least I understand how that one works.

Let's assume you're 60 and still publishing poems: what do you want to have achieved between now and then? An understanding of how Prize Bonds work would be good but, to be still alive and publishing when I'm 60? I'll take that. I like living and I like writing.

Cyril Connolly said the true function of a writer is to write a masterpiece, and no other task is of any consequence. Do you agree? Well, if you can also manage to be maimed in the Battle of Lepanto it makes for an interesting bio.

'The hard part is getting to the top of page 1' – Tom Stoppard. What, for you, is the hard part? Having to work as a teacher in order to pay bills. I like it, but if I didn't *have to* do it, I'd get to the top (and bottom) of a lot more pages.

If your ideal poem were an outfit, what would it look like? A loincloth in summer, a zoot suit in winter.

What advice would you give to older poets? Tai Chi? Aqua-aerobics? Read Walcott's 'Love after Love', feast on your life, smile more. What advice can I give older poets? Not much. Seems like there's a reason advice tends to flow in the other direction.

Is there any question you wish you'd been asked here (that you'd like to answer now?) Have you ever performed an exorcism? Yes. Yes, I have.

Sarah Clancy

THINGS I WAS THINKING WHEN SHE SAID SHE WANTED TO FEED ME
    – for Anne

I want to feed her the sting of wind burned cheeks of streaming eyes
I want to make her use that land's end too-much distance squint
I want to feel the sea-salt thickening of her hair and with her listen
to smooth stones moving against each other as the sea draws back.
I want us to shelter somewhere tin roofed and breathe in time with
the steady beat of rain, I want her to hear the low moans
an orphan wind makes at dusk when it is forced to beg for welcome
from every manmade thing, I want to offer her the discomfort flush
of wet thigh jeans or the cold-hands, warm-torso feel of Diamond Hill
or Capawalla on some blue and bracing day, I want her to welcome
the nothing feeling that comes from fossils in limestone
from ring forts' persistence or from watching the old Scots Pines
that someone planted sometime scraping at a washed out winter sky.

I want to offer her the faded votive ribbons on the naked Blackthorn
that marks the holy well, I want to feast with her on the wishes
of the unseen pilgrims who came and still come at it petitioning,
I want us to walk the pathways feral goats take at night time
and know the tangled closeness they sleep in when no one is about
I want her to see how the red-warm cattle huddle together for comfort
in their own sort of *meitheal* giving and receiving all at once
and I want to parcel these parallel worlds for her,
so that while we age in squares of love, of artificial light
and comfort, while we go about our business, we know
that outside and elsewhere things are happening without us
and I want to offer her this even if it isn't mine to give, and she,
she wants to take me in and feed me and I'm okay with this.

Sarah Clancy

CALF

Drag seaweed stalk
tall as I along the beach
plunge gulls swoop
and angry caw
wave boom fillsup
ears and mouth
further I and no one calls,
beneath-breath
salt ripe death smell pulls
to water's edge
wet black rocks
and thickstrong air,
almost sweet-almost retch
dead calf lies there stuck
goosebumps I,
at no fur shineskin,
skin creep at black tongue fat
at half moon teeth
at upper lip pulled back.
Milk-fed I bare toes curled in
stand to feed
own eyes on death
far distance someone's mother caws
for somechild,
door slam, engines brrrrr,
and I left, I left there,
poke calf with foot
then braver touch
hand palm to slimeflank,
I knees down in sand
and no one calls,
face down close, breathe deep
sweet, lost calf and I
empty summer evening beach –
I would stay till
our bones bleach.

Sarah Clancy

Were you a strange child with a taste for verse? Yes.

Do you too dislike it? I dislike lots of poetry but then when I come across a poem I like there's nothing like it. A good poem can leave a reader changed slightly, I think; reading powerful poetry is risky…

Who is your favourite character in a poem? Mrs Icarus (from the poem 'Mrs Icarus' in *The World's Wife* by Carol Ann Duffy).

If you could die and come back as a poem, what poem would it be? I would like it to be 'Animals' by Frank O'Hara but I have a feeling that it would be 'Divisions of Labour' by Adrienne Rich (again).

Someone offers you €1,000,000 to never write again: What is your response? I would take the money and assume a foolproof pseudonym.

Have you ever glued pages of a poetry book together? No?

It's the centenary of the Easter Rising: does this fact matter to you and if so, in what way? Yes, surprisingly it has mattered a good bit to me. I find the Proclamation very affecting, especially the tender fierceness of the word 'Cherish'. To look at our state now and how certain classes or categories of human are treated within it with the word cherishing in my mind is very sobering; surely we can do a bit better?

If someone described you as a political poet, what would your reaction be? In the immortal song lyrics of Skunk Anansie, 'Yes It's F***ing Political' (**https://www.youtube.com/watch?v=mcaUer4fuU8**).

Would you rather be the poet or the poem? Poet, always the poet, the poem is only one poem no matter how expansive, but the poet can write more and different poems, as many as their imagination permits.

What's your worst poetry habit? Posting poems on Facebook and then forgetting them / WRITING SHOUTY POEMS.

You've arranged a date for 8pm, but it's 8.10pm now. You're working on a poem and it's going well. What do you do? Depends on the date, and depends on the poem. I would probably keep writing though.

Have you ever carried a poem by someone else around on your person? If so, what was it? Often, most recently I think it was Kay Ryan's 'Lime Light'. I love Kay Ryan's poems.

A family member says, 'You should write a poem about that': what do you do? I roll my eyes a bit or, if feeling particularly juvenile, I'd say: 'Why don't you write it seeing as how you care that much about it.'

If your best poem were a weekend away, where would it be? In the Hotel Continental in Tangier at a windy and warm time of year.

It's a good poem but it's forty one lines long and the competition with the big prize specifies a max of forty: what do you do? Squish some lines together and not win the competition.

Have you ever used a poem to seduce someone? If so, what poem was it? (And did it work?) Is this not what they are all for? I don't think I have ever succeeded in seducing anyone with a poem, but I have definitely tried.

You're given a choice: either every poem or no poem you write from now on must use the word 'I'. Which do you choose? Every poem.

Your friend is depressed: what's the very last poetry book you'd give him / her? Anything by John Burnside – I love his writing but it aches with a desperate emptiness.

Who will play the poet in the Hollywood adaptation of your last poem? Last ever or the last poem I wrote? Robert Downey Jr., I think, or Frances McDormand.

You're invited to read in a major festival: what are your top three backstage demands? None really, maybe that the MC doesn't interrupt me half way through a poem saying 'I don't think I'd agree with you there' (this happened).

What's your current favourite word? Litany.

You're proud of the poem but know it will offend someone you don't even like: what do you do? Usually I don't write poems that are offensive to individuals, if I am ranting it is more than likely going to be about something systemic.

Would you rather win the TS Eliot Prize or the Prize Bonds? Can I not have both? Prize Bonds, then I could retire and work on my writing until I won the TS Eliot…

Let's assume you're 60 and still publishing poems: what do you want to have achieved between now and then? Just speaking of poetry, I would like to have continued to experience the fabulous feeling that comes when I am writing something that feels like a powerful or sensuous poem, and to have continued to enjoy the very rare feeling of reading or performing a poem to an audience that has completely come with you to where you were bringing them in the poem. It's indescribable but it's a kind of witchcraft that only occasionally works.

Cyril Connolly said the true function of a writer is to write a masterpiece, and no other task is of any consequence. Do you agree? No. I think writers have many functions: symbolic, practical and just general human functions. Mostly I am inclined to think that to write interestingly requires a real interest in life and that is perhaps the function I am most comfortable with or would aspire to, to really notice and see what happens and to think imaginatively and critically about it and if I am moved to do so, to write something as a result.

'The hard part is getting to the top of page 1' – Tom Stoppard. What, for you, is the hard part? Improving. I find all of it easy but don't seem to get much better.

If your ideal poem were an outfit, what would it look like? It would have loads of pockets and fit very easily. That's all I can tell you: poem = overalls?!!

What advice would you give to older poets? To stay alive for another while yet.

Jane Clarke

POINT OF DEPARTURE

A Sunday evening in January,
my father is leaving me to the train

because my mother can't; her heart
is broken over what I told her.

Just my father and me,
unused to this time together,

quiet except for the engine's hum
and the sweep of wipers

but in his silence I hear a rhythm;
he's cutting thistles with a scythe,

a gate opens
into a meadow I have never seen.

Jane Clarke

BALLYBEG

The village draws in for the night;
horse chestnut trees circling the green,
ease towards sleep while children

hang onto the swings, despite
their mother's shout, *come in out of that
or the púca will catch you,*

a couple sits close on a bench, oblivious
to everything else, someone calls *quiet*
for the weather forecast, a blackbird finishes

with a flourish. The stars have not yet
appeared but the moon, as sure as a loaf
at the back of the stove, is slowly on the rise.

Jane Clarke

Were you a strange child with a taste for verse? I wasn't conscious of liking poetry as a child but I realise now that I picked up a love of rhythm and rhyme very young, from my father quoting Hiawatha and snippets from hymns and psalms, my mother teaching me to recite poems like the 'The Owl and the Pussycat', and the songs we learned at school, such as 'Óró, sé do bheatha 'bhaile'.

Do you too dislike it? My ambivalence about poetry began in my early teens and it was only during an intense time of grief and questioning in my thirties that I found in it 'a place for the genuine'.

Who is your favourite character in a poem? The woman who speaks in Bishop's 'The Art of Losing', for her self-deprecatory humour, her music, her attempts to fool us and herself, and the terrible pathos she evokes.

If you could die and come back as a poem, what poem would it be? 'Spring' by Hopkins, because 'it strikes like lightnings to hear him sing'.

Someone offers you €1,000,000 to never write again: What is your response? No thanks – it would be like being offered a million never to feel love again.

It's the centenary of the Easter Rising: does this fact matter to you and if so, in what way? Growing up in the 1960s and '70s in a small Church of Ireland community and also being drawn to feminism and pacifism, I felt alienated from much of what was taken to be 'Irish', including pride in Easter 1916. In 2016 the reflections on the rebellion allow for a much broader range of questions, giving us an opportunity to pause and reflect on the society we have created and our visions for the future.

If someone described you as a political poet, what would your reaction be? I'd be happy that the reader sees the politics in my work, in the sense of reflecting on power and powerlessness, inclusion and exclusion, voice and voicelessness.

Would you rather be the poet or the poem? Without a doubt I'd rather be the poet; for the joy, the excitement and the magic of the making – despite the frustrations, disappointments and sense of inadequacy.

If you could pick a time to be dropped amongst the three best poets alive at that moment when would it be and who would they be? It would be the second half of the nineteenth century, when Dickinson, Hardy and Hopkins were all writing.

What's your worst poetry habit? I don't keep enough notes day-to-day of what I see, hear, feel, read, wonder, question, remember.

You've arranged a date for 8pm, but it's 8.10pm now. You're working on a poem and it's going well. What do you do? I tell myself just one minute more, just one minute more, so I can catch the last drop of that energy and then send a text and run.

Have you ever carried a poem by someone else around on your person? If so, what was it? A few years ago I decided to try to learn a poem by heart every time I went hill-walking, so I printed out Robert Frost's 'The Silken Tent'. It's still in the pocket of my walking jacket and I feel it there every time I'm out on the hills, but I haven't learned it yet.

A family member says, 'You should write a poem about that': what do you do? One of my brothers frequently comes up with ideas for the poems I should write, including one last summer about the old roof rack hanging in a shed in Roscommon. I began it tongue-in-cheek but it has become a poem I love.

If your best poem were a weekend away, where would it be? Walking in the Mournes in blue-skied, frosty weather, aware that no summits were visible yesterday in the rain and mist and that tomorrow could well be the same.

It's a good poem but it's forty-one lines long and the competition with the big prize specifies a max of forty: what do you do? I'd go at that poor poem like one of Cinderella's sisters trying to fit her foot into that small shoe.

Have you ever used a poem to seduce someone? If so, what poem was it? (And did it work?) I only began to write after I had fallen for my partner but I do think that the experience of being happily in love was part of the impulse to write poems, even though loss is a recurring theme for me.

You're given a choice: either every poem or no poem you write from now on must use the word 'I'. Which do you choose? I'd much prefer not to use 'I' at all than to have to use it in every poem. There are many ways of expressing the 'I'.

Who will play the poet in the Hollywood adaptation of your last poem? Saoirse Ronan for her talent and her gutsy, honest, down-to-earth self-possession.

What's your current favourite word? I love heft; 'That oppresses, like the Heft / Of Cathedral Tunes'.

You're proud of the poem but know it will offend someone you don't even like: what do you do? I tell myself it's impossible to know what someone else will see in a poem and then, fingers crossed, let it go.

Would you rather win the TS Eliot Prize or the Prize Bonds? Though I'd love to win the TS Eliot for a stunning collection, it's the Prize Bonds that would buy me time for all that nourishes my writing.

Let's assume you're 60 and still publishing poems: what do you want to have achieved between now and then? That's not very far away for me; I would like my writing to have developed, my poems to matter to readers and to have a second collection published.

Cyril Connolly said the true function of a writer is to write a masterpiece, and no other task is of any consequence. Do you agree? We should strive for the very best that we can do but I don't agree that it is only masterpieces that matter.

'The hard part is getting to the top of page 1' – Tom Stoppard. What, for you, is the hard part? Making it new.

If your ideal poem were an outfit, what would it look like? A ballet dancer's leotard and tights; graceful, powerful, expressive and subtly suggestive.

What advice would you give to older poets? My advice to older poets, like myself, is the same as to younger poets; keep reading, keep writing, keep learning, keep trying to get better, keep enjoying poetry and keep an openness to the world inside and outside yourself.

Adam Crothers

SLUGS

> the sky flashes, the great sea yearns
>   – John Berryman

The slug drifts from the ocean through space. As creatures do.
I take it in my grip. Others take it in the chest, I know,
or as pretext. A drone moans from the featureless blue.
A good sun in the stove of the sky. A pitiless, pilotless glow.

The evacuated street seethes in its carpet of slugs.
Glaucus atlanticus by the gross: arsenic candles
by way of memorial. The human body's a fumble of cogs
less armoured than armorial. A doodle on a sandhill.

The sight has the aroma of glaucoma when you sniff it.
The smell of the smile of the Prime Minister is the reek of
something reloading. That man is a private
island. We none of us have relatives to speak of.

One could do worse, is the horror. Some skirt
so close to the reactor that their special feelings melt.
And after a while the palmed slug can't properly hurt.
Its starship navigates the suicide belt.

Slug, you're the galaxy you cross and the gallows you're dragging!
You needn't reciprocate my wondering what you are.
It's life, friends: a glitch to which we've hitched our wagon,
a wagon worn to wreckage by that blundering star.

Life, friends: a swinger of birches, or morning stars. Counter-terror
before it hatches. The human hand, fully armed: a nail bomb.
Sail on, silver slug; steer by that firmamental error
so glaring that verily it hinders our negotiations.

As a train station's trained in frustration, so the heavenly outtake
is honed to take out evenly. The super blooper's beams are
contractually binding, penned in the demotic
in the future perfect. A footnote slips in. A miserere.

There isn't air enough. I slough off erythema
in the aspect of a dreamer, quaff folderol and oestrogen,
drinking what I can't touch. The blood of the redeemer.
Slug, the gleaming pads of my fingers are you-stricken.

The wrist's second hand is ticking. It elevates you to the light
that is, from an angle, lifting you to me, such that you're between
me and the light in this flicker-failed night and our drought-
clouded eyes swallow us until the light has nothing to see.

ON MARK HENLEY'S 'NOVEMBER SONG' AS PERFORMED BY THE FLASH GIRLS

What do these women talk about? My poems always failing
the Bechdel test, I expect. I talk about my feelings. Well, my feeling.

I feel well. I feel good. Well, I feel that I should.
I can handle the street. I get out of the woods. I get out

my clauses, which in boggy gloaming loom like the big guns.
Some cattish muse taps MUTE and tries the hedgepig wine.

That hedgepig had it coming. All inner worth must be divulged.
It should make me feel young to look so privileged.

It is, as it were, the autumn of the year. Back home we save our
sectarian burnings for the summer months. But I'm spent as a saver.

Now I own a piece of me: about as much as I can buy.
I'm not a piece of meat. My eyes are all the way

down here, where my hope-upending November song's sphere
of impudence is steamrollering every good wish, as ever.

Adam Crothers

Were you a strange child with a taste for verse? The strange thing is to retain that taste into adulthood.

Do you too dislike it? Very much so. Disliking poetry is a brilliant starting point as both a reader and a writer: if you're not automatically impressed by the notion of language being organised into lines, you'll strive harder for the good stuff.

Who is your favourite character in a poem? I wouldn't exactly wish to hang out with Porphyria's lover (from Robert Browning's 'Porphyria's Lover'), what with him being a murderer of women and all. His immense gift for sociopathic self-justification does, however, make him an invaluably educational and terrifying person with whom to spend sixty beautifully-controlled lines.

If you could die and come back as a poem, what poem would it be? One of Aram Saroyan's minimal poems. That would be lovely.

Someone offers you €1,000,000 to never write again: What is your response? 'Thanks for reading my book.'

Have you ever glued pages of a poetry book together? Nope. I once ironed a book of criticism though.

It's the centenary of the Easter Rising: does this fact matter to you and if so, in what way? Did the event matter less last year; will it matter less next year? The question of why we think centenaries are magical is an interesting one.

If someone described you as a political poet, what would your reaction be? I'd be delighted that they'd noticed that aspect of the work.

Would you rather be the poet or the poem? The poet. On the whole I like the fact that, unlike a poem, I function even when nobody's paying attention to me.

If you could pick a time to be dropped amongst the three best poets alive at that moment, when would it be and who would they be? I really shouldn't still have a romanticised view of the 1960s now that I'm in my thirties, but I do, so I'd hang out with Dylan, Larkin and Bishop in 1965, and try to keep quiet.

What's your worst poetry habit? In terms of writing, my worst habit involves saying something and then saying, as part of the poem, what

I mean, or explaining in what sense I'm using a particular word. When encountering other people's poems, my worst habit is scanning the ends of lines for rhymes before reading the poem properly.

You've arranged a date for 8pm, but it's 8.10pm now. You're working on a poem and it's going well. What do you do? I feel a little down about the fact that I've been sitting alone at the agreed venue for forty minutes and my date hasn't shown up yet.

Have you ever carried a poem by someone else around on your person? If so, what was it? I'm one of those people who feel a little uncomfortable if they don't have a book with them; so, yeah, more often than not.

A family member says, 'You should write a poem about that': what do you do? I write a poem about them saying I should write a poem about the other thing.

If your best poem were a weekend away, where would it be? Some Agatha Christie island or isolated Stephen King town where everybody's dreadful and punished.

It's a good poem but it's forty-one lines long and the competition with the big prize specifies a max of forty: what do you do? Write one more line then carve the whole effort into three sonnets. Boom! Bonus poems.

Have you ever used a poem to seduce someone? If so, what poem was it? (And did it work?) It seems I prefer to seduce people by other means and find out later that they don't really rate my poems. Fortunately it doesn't happen very often.

You're given a choice: either every poem or no poem you write from now on must use the word 'I'. Which do you choose? Oh, every poem. We're in this for the long haul, I and I.

Your friend is depressed: what's the very last poetry book you'd give him/her? As presenting a book of poems to somebody suffering from an illness, presumably in the belief that it'll fix them, strikes me as a bizarrely insensitive move, giving them my own book is the absolute worst version of such behaviour I can imagine.

Who will play the poet in the Hollywood adaptation of your last poem? That question is oddly complicated and just makes me want to watch Jason Statham kicking people, so let's say him.

You're invited to read in a major festival: what are your top three backstage demands? As long as somebody ensures that I don't get lost between the backstage and the stage, I'm happy.

What's your current favourite word? 'Entitlement'. I work in an academic library so I mutter it a lot.

You're proud of the poem but know it will offend someone you don't even like: what do you do? Celebrate.

Would you rather win the TS Eliot Prize or the Prize Bonds? I don't think I'm tough enough to cope with winning the Eliot and having people with no previously stated interest in poetry attempt to figure out why I didn't deserve to. At least they wouldn't be racist or sexist about it in my case.

Let's assume you're 60 and still publishing poems: what do you want to have achieved between now and then? That sounds like all I could reasonably hope to achieve.

Cyril Connolly said the true function of a writer is to write a masterpiece, and no other task is of any consequence. Do you agree? This is the bit where he said that otherwise you might as well be peeling potatoes, yes? Paul Muldoon wrote a good poem about this for the now sadly static website *Quickmuse*. Potatoes, literal or otherwise, do often need to be peeled.

'The hard part is getting to the top of page 1' – Tom Stoppard. What, for you, is the hard part? Ensuring that the finished poem makes some sense without eradicating the mystery and energy and noise and indeed nonsense that made the first draft happen.

If your ideal poem were an outfit, what would it look like? An obvious hand-me-down.

What advice would you give to older poets? Assuming that 'older' implies 'more established', I'd suggest that they try very hard not to consider themselves great philosophers in possession of unprecedented insight: they're still primarily in the business of arranging syllables, and that responsibility shouldn't be shirked.

Is there any question you wish you'd been asked here (that you'd like to answer now?) Q: How have the American versions of Gordon Ramsay's cookery shows influenced your writing over the last few years? A: I'm afraid the word limit makes it impossible to answer this question sufficiently.

Paula Cunningham

MORE OR LESS
   – for Paul

What you told me in the multi-
storied car park of the Maldron,
those liquid hours when smoke
and talk prevail, is hazy now
but vivid too for me.
                    The shutter,
if you timed it right, you'd roll
in under to a clean, safe place –
the bank's al fresco foyer,
where half-smoked butts
employees stubbed would yield
enough tobacco for a week –
                         how often,
in interminable illness,
I would have given anything
for that.

Paula Cunningham

THE MAGNETIC HILL

Good Sundays we would rise
for early Mass and pack a picnic
for the Gortin Glens –
our crammed car passed Tircur's
abandoned schoolhouse
where weekly he would vow
to leave his daughters.

At the brow of the hill he'd cut
the engine, free-wheel
halfway down and stop,
release the brake and pause,
hands-off, then crawl
back up as the fields fed out
while the sheep and the lambs fed on.

This time last year he was still
alive, and a stopped car
sails back uphill yet, amassing
speed as the fields roll by.

Paula Cunningham

Were you a strange child with a taste for verse? I was a strange child with a taste for boiled ham and Lovehearts. I was eating words from an early age. I liked rhymes and skipping songs. I loved dictionaries, and kept a vocabulary notebook. At home I discovered tone of voice, how it subverted meaning. I went to Irish dancing lessons in Omagh. Charlie Reilly played the fiddle live for our classes. It was an apprenticeship in rhythm. You couldn't hear those tunes and remain still. They'd marvellous names like 'Planxty Drury', 'Cherish the Ladies' and 'Hurry the Jug'.

The verse came very much later. That said, I did enjoy the 3rd Eucharistic Prayer at Mass, and was always disappointed when the priest chose another version. I wasn't religious so I'm guessing it was the language and rhythms of that particular prayer which the other versions lacked.

Who is your favourite character in a poem? I like Philip Larkin's Mr Bleaney, and the first-person speaker in Edna St Vincent Millay's sonnets. Also the characters Matthew Sweeney creates – his blending of the comical, the bizarre, the philosophical.

Someone offers you €1,000,000 to never write again: What is your response? Can you make that Sterling?

Have you ever glued pages of a poetry book together? I got through a couple of paperback copies of Kahlil Gibran's *The Prophet* in my late teens. I've a Sellotaped copy somewhere in the house.

It's the centenary of the Easter Rising: does this fact matter to you and if so, in what way? I've the memoirs of a great-uncle, a young priest in Dublin in 1916. There's mention of firearms secreted in the sacristy. I like that juxtaposition, though it brings to mind other unholy juxtapositions our religious institutions seem particularly prone to.

If someone described you as a political poet, what would your reaction be? I'd have some difficulty with that; poetry and politics don't necessarily make good bedfellows. I'm leery of the didactic in the political. I dislike being told what to think, especially in a poem. I do like poetry of witness though, 'just what happened and our watching it' (Kevin Power, *The Yellow Birds*). And nature poetry, nowadays, is inevitably political. Of course it could be argued that all poetry is political insofar as it's a minority sport, is counter-cultural, and has little, if any, pecuniary value. Labels like 'political poet' can be immensely limiting; I dislike labels of every stripe and hate to see people being pigeonholed in any way.

Would you rather be the poet or the poem? I'd rather be alive; the poem is only alive for as long as it's being read.

What's your worst poetry habit? Maurice Riordan describes himself as a 'binge poet', and the term resonates for me. Occasionally I regret not making more time to read and write.

You've arranged a date for 8pm, but it's 8.10pm now. You're working on a poem and it's going well. What do you do? That would depend on the calibre and potential of the date. 'There are things that are important beyond all this fiddle'.

Have you ever carried a poem by someone else around on your person? If so, what was it? I carry poems around a fair bit as I do some facilitation with community groups. I like to start by looking at, and discussing, one or two exemplary poems. It always raises the game; the responses rarely fail to educate and astonish. I had Richard Murphy's 'Moonshine' in my wallet a few years back. I must have been feeling ambivalent.

I suppose memorising poems, or lines, would be equivalent to carrying the poems around *in* your person. Paula Meehan's 'Fruit' springs to mind, as does Carol Rumens' 'The Hag of Beare in Limerick' and Anon's 'I eat my peas with honey'. I have a terrible memory and these are very short. I still remember Oliver Goldsmith's slightly longer 'When Lovely Woman Stoops to Folly' and MacNeice's 'Autumn Journal', Section IV. I know poets who carry small libraries in their heads – John Brown and Sinéad Morrissey both have this enviable capacity.

Then there are the poems which make what Michael Longley calls 'the envy gland' throb, and those that burrow under your skin and produce a chronic pruritus – Catherine Wing's 'The Darker Sooner', from *Best American Poetry 2010*, has been an irritant for years.

It's a good poem but it's forty-one lines long and the competition with the big prize specifies a max of forty: what do you do? Chop. Submitting always makes my poems wobble, like the icons on an iPhone. It usually happens immediately after I've hit 'Send'. The poem comes into new focus under that pressure. It's always a good opportunity to re-revise.

Reader, I've done this. The poem ran up.

Have you ever used a poem to seduce someone? If so, what poem was it? (And did it work?) It could only ever be Louis MacNeice's 'Autumn Journal', Section IV: 'September has come and I wake ...'

You're given a choice: either every poem or no poem you write from now on must use the word 'I'. Which do you choose? One would write what one wanted, or needed, or was otherwise compelled to write. One would feel duty-bound to defy any such edict. That said, constraint is a friend to the writer.

What's your current favourite word? Thran.

You're proud of the poem but know it will offend someone you don't even like: what do you do? Agonise. Publish. Agonise.

Let's assume you're 60 and still publishing poems: what do you want to have achieved between now and then? Another collection, the Prize Bonds. Some short stories. To have become a better teacher. To be healthy and content, better-travelled and better-read.

Cyril Connolly said the true function of a writer is to write a masterpiece, and no other task is of any consequence. Do you agree? A masterpiece is the culmination of many steps. The steps are worthy of consideration in their own right whether or not a masterpiece transpires. (Who is to judge?)

'The hard part is getting to the top of page 1' – Tom Stoppard. What, for you, is the hard part? Ditto. Knowing when to stop the infernal fiddling.

If your ideal poem were an outfit, what would it look like? It would be home-made from local materials, timeless, and not inelegant. It would be comprised of numerous layers, much like filo pastry, though this would not be immediately apparent. The fabric would be static-prone and flammable, silent at rest, but liable to rustle pleasingly in light winds. It would function as a semi-permeable membrane, much like the blood-brain barrier, but capricious. It would be iridescent, responsive to light and heat, and emit a faint glow in the dark. The fabric would quickly saturate in wet conditions but dry almost instantaneously. It would be odourless, yielding delicate hints of grapefruit and gooseberry when licked. The taste would subtly alter with subsequent licks, and no two lickers would ever agree entirely on the flavour.

Ailbhe Darcy

MARTINSTAG

Our paper lanterns are not flares but sparks
off some imagined bonfire while somewhere

Europe dreams of burning, dreams of bombs
that will be sent off here and there, piercing

light, their history a history of staring
into fire. Europe dreams of burning,

dreams of bombs. A bomb is made, in part,
of light, of visits to the cinema, where Paris,

made of light, must be annihilated first.
Our lanterns are not flares but sparks.

Here the harvest's in, the children witness
to corn's absence in the field, the quince trees

stripped of all their quinces. Europe dreams of
burning, dreams of bombs. We sing and see

St Martin on his horse, a vision of the strangeness
little children swim in, beneath the light of stars.

Beneath the stars, the light of us. Our paper lanterns,
swinging as we walk, are not flares but sparks

off some imagined bonfire while somewhere
Europe dreams of burning, dreams of bombs.

Ailbhe Darcy

HONK FOR PEACE

Balloon animals everywhere at the La Porte County Fair that one
    Sunday.
A balloon monkey halfway up a balloon tree,
balloon Dalmatian pelicans, a balloon dragonfly with dogged felt tip
    marker eyes.

Me snarfing elephant ears nasty with sugar, you steak tips as usual,
our son petitioning for a balloon spider. What he got (and he'll take
what he gets) was a balloon squid, pulled it along behind him like a
    pet.

It balloon shivered. We saw The Strangest Thing. Balloon dogs
turned balloon tricks. Driving home we drove past protesters.
You wouldn't honk the horn, still insisting,

'Shouldn't we present a strong response to chemical weapons?'
down through all the years, as if I hadn't won the argument circa 2006.
I'll think too late, triumphant: But America can't afford

a response! (We don't pay our soldiers). Then, undoing it:
but of course we wouldn't want to wake the boy, honking like loons.

The boy: sticky with lemon shake-up in the back seat, worn out
petting all those ponies. The balloons: cleaving the air in their free
flight, feeling its resistance.

Ailbhe Darcy

Were you a strange child with a taste for verse? Wasn't everybody? My son at three is peculiar as a red-lipped batfish, and, looking around at his kindergarten colleagues, he's hardly alone. All quite bats and all moony in love with words. These children perform feats of rhythm and word-play – quite absent-mindedly, while playing with toy cars or trains – at which we grown-ups can only swoon. As for my son's taste in verse, he recognizes Shirley Hughes's *Out and About* for the masterpiece it is, but refuses to acknowledge the dud notes in the other Hughes's *Moon-Whales*. So I have hope for many a heated debate between us in the future.

When I was a bit older than him, I spent hours with *Talking to the Sun*, a gorgeous anthology which pairs poems with paintings from the Met Museum. A book which values strangeness and doesn't pretend to have all the answers. It made me feel that there was a gravity to this world of art and poetry that nothing else in life approached. I don't know what age I was when I rolled my eyes and told my Dad scornfully, 'poems don't have to *rhyme* you know,' but I've never lived it down.

Do you too dislike it? My long-suffering husband is witness to the fact that, in the dark times, I wail 'but I don't even *like* poems!' Neither of us knows what I intend by that.

Who is your favourite character in a poem? At the time of writing, Action Man in Jennifer L Knox's 'Cue: "Action Man" Theme'. 'He's so hyper-vigilant!'

If you could die and come back as a poem, what poem would it be? Can I be Keats's 'This living hand, now warm and capable'? Put the heebie-jeebies up everyone?

Someone offers you €1,000,000 to never write again: What is your response? I think I've already answered that question by dint of the life I'm leading. No one ever dangled a large cheque, but I could have taken a more practical route than writing and scholarship towards, say, a pension, home ownership, regular haircuts. It's not like I didn't know that. But what I've always really wanted, top priority, is something to write about and time to write it.

Yes, the older I get, the more I value small comforts like washing machines and tumble dryers, free-range chickens and proper healthcare. The older I get, the more I would stammer and twitch while turning down the million. The more I would need a stiff drink afterwards. But I'd still say: 'Thanks all the same – I couldn't interest you in paying me to write at all?'

It's the centenary of the Easter Rising: does this fact matter to you and if so, in what way? The fact of the Easter Rising matters to me. Its theatricality, the way it conjured a Republic out of thin air, gives me hope that we might yet have the gumption and wherewithal to construct an idea of Ireland that would do us all proud. If a commemoration can inspire us, I'm all for it. At a remove, though, it's hard to be inspired. The victory for gay marriage was explosive, but I haven't seen much else exciting coming out of Ireland of late.

If someone described you as a political poet, what would your reaction be? As far as I know, aspiring to be a political poet is the exact same thing as aspiring to be a poet. It's the whole game. If someone described me as succeeding, I'd be flattered, then I'd be abashed and then I'd feel like a fraud, because I know I'm not there yet.

If anything, I worry the events of my life over the last few years have conspired to quench the political fire in my poetry. I'm a middle-class em-igrant with a European passport in my greedy mitt, so I'm extraordinarily privileged but I'm also disenfranchised: I feel confusingly distant from any political reality. Meanwhile, as a mother with limited means, I struggle to find time and energy for my writing. When I do, it's my own life I yearn to think through in my poems – since the birth of my son, I've felt tied up in knots. So I fret that the scope of my work has shrunk. When I finished my first collection, Kevin Higgins wrote me a blurb which said, 'Never self-absorbed, she is a poet consumed by what the world around her is doing', and that generous description haunts me, goads me.

If you could pick a time to be dropped amongst the three best poets alive at that moment, when would it be and who would they be? There is just one poet I wish I could have met, and that's Dorothy Molloy. She died in 2004, when her first collection was at press. I wonder what she was like at twenty-one, in 1963. Make the two of us twenty-one, why not? And drop us in New York for double-date cocktails with two bad old men, Frank O'Hara and Kenneth Koch.

What's your worst poetry habit? Typing the poem up too soon. I write in longhand, draft after draft, and each draft is a little better. If only I could keep doing that indefinitely! Twenty years, forty! Then, *then* might I con-jure a poem as cold and passionate as the dawn! But sooner or later I get all excited about what a poem's going to look like on the page, and next thing I know the blaster is in a word processing file and I'm not writing anymore, I'm editing. Then there's only so much better it can get.

Who will play the poet in the Hollywood adaptation of your last poem? Richard E Grant. Ah no. Paul McGann.

What's your current favourite word? Giftschrank. German for your medicine cabinet, your liquor cabinet or your porn stash.

Cyril Connolly said the true function of a writer is to write a masterpiece, and no other task is of any consequence. Do you agree? Not at all. What matters is the body of work built up over time, the record of a lifetime's thought and practice.

If your ideal poem were an outfit, what would it look like? With the advance on my first collection I actually did buy a dress. It's creamy, belted, printed with leaves and cheeky-eyed birds in autumnal colours. The stitching is all on the outside, where you can see it. My ideal poem would be like my dress: hard-earned, easy on the eye, paying tribute to formal tradition but not hung up on it. And something you can rely on at intense moments. My dress has never let me down. I wore it the night before I got married, armour against the nerves.

What advice would you give to older poets? Don't type the poem up too soon. Buy a nice dress. Keep saying no to the million euros.

Is there any question you wish you'd been asked here (that you'd like to answer now?) What poem should we play at your funeral? Dream Song 14. 'Life, friends, is boring...'

Lisa O'Donnell

The Dorchester House
Oil on linen, 30 cm x 22 cm

W. www.lisaodonnellartist.com

Lisa O'Donnell

Nora
Oil on linen, 30 cm x 22 cm

W. www.lisaodonnellartist.com

Lisa O'Donnell

You Can't Beat an Education
Oil on linen, 30 cm x 22 cm

W. www.lisaodonnellartist.com

Lisa O'Donnell

100 and 1
Oil on canvas, 46 cm x 41 cm

W. www.lisaodonnellartist.com

Naomi Vona

Light Spaceship
Pen on vintage photo, 12.3 cm x 7.5 cm

Naomi Vona

Forgot Saint
Collage, 7 in x 5 in

W. www.saatchiart.com/naomivona

Naomi Vona

Precious Things
Collage, 11 in x 7.7 in

Naomi Vona

Uno, Nessuno e Centomila, Mini Series 001
Collage, 5.4 in x 3.3 in

W. www.saatchiart.com/naomivona

Martin Dyar

BREAD AND MILK

What they found in Galway proved addictive.
It's strange to say that now, but no other
word quite holds the darkness they would reach
through those weekly Connemara retreats.

After the dabbling phase, there was scarcely
a Friday that they did not flee Dublin
direct from work, both of them helplessly
focussed on the bread of that seclusion,

and on the milk of how their souls behaved
in the wordless, oblivion-powered work
of their wholly indescribable sex games.
We judge them now, and lament them, because

it went so wrong. But, early on, we saw
only the blaze of eccentricities
that lit their single-minded journey west
and not their bid for God in nothingness.

Martin Dyar

THE PLOT

There was a plot to keep Anne in Dublin.
Five ex-boyfriends, myself the driving force,
met up for drinks and fed each other's need
to pin her down this time and make her see.

County Sligo, we'd heard, was in her mind.
And none would underestimate the draw.
Sligo, with those wide, butter-armoured dunes,
those copper-brained, summer-defying lakes,

where nature waives self meteorologically
and Donegal eagles mark Nordic time –
all this mirrored Anne's personality.
We drank her health and cursed her dream of peace.

But our sad friendships were subjective prey
to the drug of being Anne's man once again.
And so it came to nothing, except this:
she left us, Sligo won, she farms there now.

But today there's a primal photo in the *Times*.
A juvenile fox held in Anne's long arms.
I have read entrancedly, and now I weep
across the organic face of endless love.

Martin Dyar

Were you a strange child with a taste for verse? I might well have been.
Through my teens poetry was hand in hand with sport. It's heartening
to look back and to consider the strangeness of that leaning, and to think
of something woken there, something at once innocent and serious. In
the poem 'Sanctity', Patrick Kavanagh has that wonderful line (infused
with his special brand of anguish): 'To be a poet and not know the trade'.
To have had a period of innocence in relation to poetry, to have had an
unsponsored desire for it, is a valuable thing to carry, for the times when
encouragement and innocence are in short supply.

Who is your favourite character in a poem? My favourite character is Reuben
Bright, in the poem 'Reuben Bright' by Edwin Arlington Robinson. He
lives within one of my favourite sonnets, like a caretaker, and his story
preserves a humane image of rage against time and loss, along with an
unforgettable image of love.

If you could die and come back as a poem, what poem would it be? I would
choose 'The Owl in the Sarcophagus' by Wallace Stevens. Previous lives;
spirals of metempsychosis; being an animal one minute and an element
the next; doors in and out of heaven; eternity as sense experience – these
things are mere starting points in the world of that fabulous poem. I
imagine it would be a good place to come to terms with a metamorphosis.
It might also hold an added peace, since many critics dislike the poem. I'd
be left to my own devices. You couldn't wish to be a poem without wish-
ing to be misunderstood.

Someone offers you €1,000,000 to never write again: What is your response?
Wasn't there a television ad where a busker was offered money on the
condition that he stop performing? It's a thing to ponder, though the
answer for most poets is probably the same: no. If such demonic philan-
thropy existed, it would be interesting to study and compare the countries,
and to see which poetry territory had the highest numbers of people
willing to go silent. Wallace Stevens once said that money is a kind of
poetry. I think he meant that there is something we feel in our dreams of
wealth, in our lottery salivations, which belongs to the sphere of essential
happiness, and that that feeling does not in the least belong to money,
although money prompts it. The writing of poetry can provide a sense of
invigoration which might be compared to a kind of cash, a kind of return.
Now and again such experiences amount to windfalls of vision and voice,
and they can lead to the personal pricelessness of a good poem. Maybe
the thing to hope for here is to escape certain benefactors.

It's the centenary of the Easter Rising: does this fact matter to you and if so, in what way? Our history is a deep well, and around the well is a great place to gather. There's courting and flattery and music and food, and the best of guff is in the air. In poetry terms, Ireland itself is a great subject, and this year many great poems come at us like comets across the century, bearing the best of instincts, the best of questions. But of course, in the knowledge of the gap between the official and the real Ireland, many of our dead writers will continue to turn in their graves. Some of them are probably turning like lathes.

Have you ever carried a poem by someone else around on your person? If so, what was it? 'The Ram's Horn' by John Hewitt has served as a kind of hip-flask. And also the lyrics to the song 'Red Apples' by Bill Callahan.

A family member says, 'You should write a poem about that': what do you do? I feel rallied to a state of misgiving and percolation which will last for two or three years, before eventually leading to a mutated form of the original idea in an unrelated poem.

What's your current favourite word? My current favourite word is 'Mermaidism'.

Cyril Connolly said the true function of a writer is to write a masterpiece, and no other task is of any consequence. Do you agree? This reminds me of Yeats's words in the poem 'Ego Dominus Tuus': 'I seek an image, not a book.' In most cases, talk of a commitment to making poetic masterpieces probably means that perfectionism and procrastination (those warty partners) have taken full possession of the mind. Having said that, poetry does permit a slow approach and the pursuit of a fuller integration of elements, in ways that novels and plays perhaps do not.

What advice would you give to older poets? I would like to pass on Jack Kerouac's eccentric bit of encouragement: 'You're a Genius all the time'.

Let's assume you're 60 and still publishing poems: what do you want to have achieved between now and then? Happily, sixty is youngish in Ireland these days, and it's getting younger. I'm hoping I'll have written some poems that reflect aspects of the depth and pleasure of a poetry journey. I hope too that my sixty-year-old self will not be living too much in the past. I might read these very words on my sixtieth birthday, so perhaps I should say now, 'Don't look back, you fool.' There's a wonderful moment in Rilke's poem 'Orpheus. Eurydice. Hermes.' Orpheus has chanted his way into the underworld and bargained for his love Eurydice's release. Now he has the task of hiking back up to the surface, while directly behind him the messenger god Hermes leads Eurydice along in the darkness. It has been agreed that they will have another life together if Orpheus manages not to look back during the ascent. He copes fairly well with the challenge at first, but then, tormented by the fear that his love is no longer following him, he turns around. Here Rilke adds a magnificently poignant touch. Eurydice is too deep in her death for revival, which suggests that if Orpheus had fulfilled the task their reunion might still have been doomed. The gods must have known this. When Hermes sees that Orpheus has looked back, he officiously raises his cloak and turns to lead Eurydice away from the light. By way of instructing her to return to the belly of the earth with him, he tells her simply: 'He has turned around'. And then Rilke puts one word in drowsy Eurydice's mouth. She asks, 'Who?'

My favourite closing lines of any book are in John Banville's novel *Athena*. The lines are: ' "Write to me," she said. "Write to me." I have written.' That for me captures something of how it feels to want to do this. There's a gorgeous invisibility, and she keeps repeating herself. Write to me, write to me. If I make it to sixty I hope I will hear a few notes in her voice which suggest some of my words have hit home. In the meantime, I hope I have heard her correctly.

Elaine Gaston

ALLOTMENT

My grandmother checks her onion sets,
hokes down into the rich crumble of compost
that she turned with her own hand.

Soil made from vegetable peel, eggshells, newspaper.
She chooses an onion for the stew,
chops it with carrots, her own home-grown spuds.

It's not the spider's web on the gorse bush,
the hawthorn hedge at the edge of the top field,
how it became the new motorway,

it's not the tiny, shiny green beetles
that she hunkered to watch as a child, their vanishing,
miniscule lives as important as anyone's,

or fewer swallows this year, the way they gather,
all dinner jackets and fork-tails on the telegraph wire,
then swoop for midges over the salmon pools up the glen.

It's not even the deletion of *conker*, *bluebell*, *acorn*
or *blackberry*, or the way our neighbours
in Donegal sat on the sofa looking at television

when she thought they were watching
the sunset out their picture window.
It's when she takes all these things together.

When she sees it all pared back, layer by layer,
the way she peels the onion – it never seems to end,
yet suddenly it has no centre, is no longer there –

that is the thing she watches for.

Elaine Gaston

THE CLOUGHMILLS WATER

There was a heat-wave all that summer.
He was fifteen years old at the time.
He worked all day on the farm
then slipped off after dinner,
a towel and a rope under his arm.

He stripped off his workclothes
slipped a reef knot around the fence post,
the other end around his waist,
then waded into the claggy water.
Stones jagged his bare feet, mud sucked his toes

as he dared himself in.
His breath caught with the chill of it.
The river pulled and tugged his limbs.
He ducked his head under, sliced his arms,
waded out to where the floor was smoother,

lifted one foot off, then the other,
thrashed and kicked, tested the water,
shouted with the thrill of it,
dived down to touch the sandy bed
while the rope and river held.

Elaine Gaston

Were you a strange child with a taste for verse? I've always loved rhymes and verse of any kind. The teacher at our small, rural primary school entered us for choral speaking in the Feis. I can still remember the thrill of a group speaking as one. It felt like a living, breathing being. We also learned by heart and recited poems for family, school concerts or community gatherings. My parents and teachers encouraged a love of poetry as part of life. Not as something odd or extra. My parents had learned poetry at school and it stayed in their minds. I don't think it was unusual. The rhythms of those early poems have always stayed with me.

Do you too dislike it? I will always love words.

Who is your favourite character in a poem? I think June Jordan's DeLiza poems and Jackie Kay's Maw Broon poems are great. They are meaningful and witty at the same time.

If you could die and come back as a poem, what poem would it be? The first stanza of Christina Rossetti's 'In the Bleak Midwinter'. I have known that stanza since I was a very young child. I could recite it or sing it for ages, over and over again. I find it endlessly fascinating, with many layers, like the snow that suffuses it. It has a great mixture of simplicity, concrete images and sounds as well as having a spiritual dimension. It is also amazing how she uses the word 'snow' five times, each time with a slightly different meaning. All in four short lines. It makes bleak magical.

Someone offers you €1,000,000 to never write again: What is your response? It's not about the money!

Have you ever glued pages of a poetry book together? No, but I once worked in a library which contained first-edition poetry books by early twentieth-century Irish women. The pages were not yet cut. I'd still love to know what was in those pages.

It's the centenary of the Easter Rising: does this fact matter to you and if so, in what way? Yes it does. Two of my grandparents were from Dublin and alive then. I was fortunate that my grandfather lived to a very old age so I was able to ask him about 1916. I wish now that I had asked him more. I also had a great-uncle on my northern side who was in the Somme and died at Ypres a few years later. So 1916 means many things to me in many ways. It seemed like ancient history when I was a child, but now it seems so close in time. And it means more to me as the years go by.

Would you rather be the poet or the poem? Can I be both?

If you could pick a time to be dropped amongst the three best poets alive at that moment, when would it be and who would they be? Now is a great time. But if it was back in time, then the late 1960s, early 1970s: June Jordan, Seamus Heaney, Pablo Neruda.

What's your worst poetry habit? Writing in different notebooks, whatever I have to hand, then having to search for something to finish it. It wastes time. But then sometimes it leads me to re-read something else I wrote and forgot about. So it can work both ways.

You've arranged a date for 8pm, but it's 8.10pm now. You're working on a poem and it's going well. What do you do? Keep the date of course!

Have you ever carried a poem by someone else around on your person? If so, what was it? I had a newspaper clipping of Seamus Heaney's 'Postscript' on my wall when I lived in England. I also had a beautiful copy of June Jordan's poem 'Free Flight' pinned up in the kitchen of a shared house. I have a copy of Sinéad Morrissey's 'Genetics' on my noticeboard at work, it's been there for a few years.

A family member says, 'You should write a poem about that': what do you do? I don't!

It's a good poem but it's forty-one lines long and the competition with the big prize specifies a max of forty: what do you do? I don't really write poems for competitions and rarely have one that would suit a competition. Lines change all the time when I am writing a poem and they often get chopped when I am editing. However in a finished poem the line should have earned its place enough to stay. If not, it should be cut anyway.

You're given a choice: either every poem or no poem you write from now on must use the word 'I'. Which do you choose? Using the first person can give a lot of scope. The speaker can be anyone, so there is a lot of potential to explore strong and diverse characters very powerfully.

You're invited to read in a major festival: what are your top three backstage demands? Backstage sounds good enough!

What's your current favourite word? Sweltered.

Would you rather win the TS Eliot Prize or the Prize Bonds? I'm doing well if I win a Christmas raffle!

Let's assume you're 60 and still publishing poems: what do you want to have achieved between now and then? I'd love to keep writing and complete more collections. I also love collaborating with other artists and hope to make more theatre and dance pieces. On the personal side I'd like to be kind, loving and do the right thing.

Cyril Connolly said the true function of a writer is to write a masterpiece, and no other task is of any consequence. Do you agree? Did he? Well, you can't beat great writing. But I think it is also important not to be selfish, to live a good life in the world and to be loving.

'The hard part is getting to the top of page 1' – Tom Stoppard. What, for you, is the hard part? Honestly, the hard part for me is knowing when a piece is finished. That and actually getting around to sending work out.

If your ideal poem were an outfit, what would it look like? Probably different every time, depending on the season and occasion. I like bright colours and putting together my own outfits. Sometimes these are fairly straight-forward, sometimes more individual. I like some surprise, large or small: a piece of unusual jewellery or a scarf. It's how things are put together by a particular person that make an outfit work. Like a poem.

What advice would you give to older poets? I take advice from them! I would like to thank them.

Is there any question you wish you'd been asked here (that you'd like to answer now?) I would like to pay tribute to Joan Newmann. She was one of the few Northern women having poetry published in 1960s Belfast. She opened the door for others. She inspired and continues to inspire many people.

Eleanor Hooker

STORM SONG

The autumn line-storm bears the lake
to my door, and in the pounding water
is my menagerie of three-eyed fish, and in the
ardent air – an arabesque of ravens and rooks.

This porous house has never resisted,
the wind unknots and all rain in.
Once inside, my fishes and the birds
resume their routine of swim and storm song.

I find breathing space on a bloated chest,
rise to the rafters with a raven and a rook
beside me, monitoring the flood. Attic curtains
spinnaker, and the house runs before the wind.

In large dense shoals, my fish dive free
to the deepest available water, drawing
down the broken echoes of my humming,
sending back up the stormy shadows of my song.

Eleanor Hooker

THE SHELTERED WORLD

We navigate the narrow neck
of darkness to find them in the gut
of the night – fouled, stricken, wrecked.
We return them to the sheltered world,

and in returning to the sheltered world
we sup at the Still, our land-legs hollow
but restless to put to sea restored.
Cradling a carafe of light, an ancient seafarer

crosses the bar to take up station
beside us. He declares he's glad
we're here, glad we fetched them back
alive, says 'twas different in the auld times.

In the auld times, he says, 'twas different –
on nights such as this they dragged
a grapnel along the grey water's bed,
and often as not snagged the afterworld.

Along the grey water's bed their grapnel
rent unanswered prayers, unused flares,
a mother's dream as they hooked her child
and brought him, punctured, to the surface.

Eleanor Hooker

Were you a strange child with a taste for verse? Strange, perhaps, but not because I had a taste for verse. After supper I would stand by Dad, sing or recite my day to everyone round the table. It didn't much matter if I were tuneless or rhyme-less; the object was to make everyone smile. Laughter was a bonus.

Someone offers you €1,000,000 to never write again: What is your response? I'd hire a stenographer, adopt a pose, and begin dictation.

Have you ever glued pages of a poetry book together? No. Truth is, I've yet to find a book of poetry I've disliked enough to glue its pages together, no wait, I lie, there is *one*.

It's the centenary of the Easter Rising: does this fact matter to you and if so, in what way? I first learned about the Easter Rising as a child, from my grandfather. He played an active role in the events in Kerry. As a child I didn't understand the impact it had on him, for me it was just another story. He said terrible things happened during and after the Rising.

Peter's family offered their home as a safe house, a dangerous move for Protestant Irish. Our grandparents believed in fairness and justice. My personal hope is that the commemorations don't awaken old hatreds and enmities.

If someone described you as a political poet, what would your reaction be? It would depend very much on who was speaking. I've no desire to be categorised or labelled. For me, that old adage applies, 'the personal is political'.

Would you rather be the poet or the poem? The poet. Imagine having to live with these cryptic, final two lines for all eternity. 'Beauty is truth, truth beauty, – that is all / Ye know on earth, and all ye need to know.'

If you could pick a time to be dropped amongst the three best poets alive at that moment, when would it be and who would they be? I would love to have a free pass to a 1970s weekend-long seminar on poetry and the philosophy of poetry by Tomas Tranströmer, Inger Christensen and Galway Kinnell.

What's your worst poetry habit? Doubt. Self-censorship.

You've arranged a date for 8pm, but it's 8.10pm now. You're working on a poem and it's going well. What do you do? Explain to my husband the 'date' is with the girls, explain to the girls that I'm on the cusp of a line break, to drop round 'bout ten, that mulled wine will be ready by the campfire.

Have you ever carried a poem by someone else around on your person? If so, what was it? Yes, Michael Hartnett's 'The Naked Surgeon'. It's a difficult poem, about the creative process, outsider-ness, despair, self-destruction and ultimately, hope, all phrased in the most exquisite lines of poetry. This poem works for me on so many levels. 'I was called, no scalpel packed. / I threw a saddle on the dark / and galloped to the threshold of his mind.'

A family member says, 'You should write a poem about that': what do you do? Make a note never to write a poem about that thing. Years later, write a poem about that thing.

If your best poem were a weekend away, where would it be? Back in the Sequoia National Park, amongst the giant Redwoods. I'd even keep the brown bear that galumphed across the meadow towards us, at Tharp's Log.

It's a good poem but it's forty-one lines long and the competition with the big prize specifies a max of forty: what do you do? I'd definitely review the poem, if an edit didn't diminish it in any way, I'd edit. If losing a line compromised the poem, I'd enter another poem.

Have you ever used a poem to seduce someone? If so, what poem was it? (And did it work?) Yes. Thomas Kinsella's poem 'Midsummer'. Yes, it worked. 'The evening is a huge closed door / And no one sees / / How we, absorbed in our own art, / Have locked ourselves inside one heart ...'

You're given a choice: either every poem or no poem you write from now on must use the word 'I'. Which do you choose? Tiffany Atkinson's poem 'Autobiography Without Pronouns' is wonderfully impressive. Great poems are written without the use of the perpendicular pronoun. Still, I'd refuse to make this choice as it would adversely affect my poetry.

Your friend is depressed: what's the very last poetry book you'd give him/her? Philip Schultz, *Failure*, a delightful collection, but that title...

Who will play the poet in the Hollywood adaptation of your last poem? Helena Bonham Carter.

You're invited to read in a major festival: what are your top three backstage demands? Could you imagine being that brattish, mortifying.

What's your current favourite word? Werifesteria – 'to wander longingly through the forest in search of adventure'.

You're proud of the poem but know it will offend someone you don't even like: what do you do? Keep the poem. It has something to say and might be the most honest poem in the file.

Would you rather win the TS Eliot Prize or the Prize Bonds? As I still have my windfall after interpreting question 2 to the letter, the TS Eliot please.

Let's assume you're 60 and still publishing poems: what do you want to have achieved between now and then? Remain healthy.

Cyril Connolly said the true function of a writer is to write a masterpiece, and no other task is of any consequence. Do you agree? Cyril Connolly also said, 'Better to write for yourself and have no public, than to write for the public and have no self.' Readers decide if a book is a masterpiece, not the writer, the writer hopes their book will be warmly received. 'Masterpiece' might be a word drained of any real meaning by being overused.

'The hard part is getting to the top of page 1' – Tom Stoppard. What, for you, is the hard part? Editing, without breaking the poem into tiny glass splinters.

If your ideal poem were an outfit, what would it look like? A bodice of raven feathers, a skirt of rain, lake water and fish scales, back buttoned with fresh green acorns.

What advice would you give to older poets? Age, it's just a number. Here's a mathematical proof my son William has given to me that age is just a number.

Mark Twain once said: 'Age is just a case of mind over matter: If you don't mind, then it doesn't matter.' Therefore: Age = Mind / Matter.

But, your mind is just composed of grey matter, so: Mind = Grey x Matter.

For most of us however, this concept is a grey area. Therefore: Grey = Area. So: Age = Mind / Matter = (Grey x Matter) / Matter
$\qquad$ = (Area x Matter) / Matter = Area.

But hey, area is just a number, right? Therefore: Age = Number, for most of us!

Caoilinn Hughes

COMPLAINTS PROCEDURE

We need to talk about your hands.
Leave it alone. They're grand.
They're fruitcakes, plum-flecked technicolour arras.
Arragh. He tsks. Swats the conversation with his palm.
I'll not be calmed by the nurse's tip that the spots
'can be froze for months on end and they'll keep.'
I spent my youth under the fitful sun out in them acres
and those damn tubers bulge up from the muck
and latch like dawn. Never bedevilled the body
in sunblock for I didn't mean to stay so long –
that squelch and slap of working leech-loam
wasn't how I'd planned to trudge a way ahead.
I wouldn't build my home from turf.
But I did build it with these hands.

We need to talk about your scalp.
I had the lot of it gouged out and it's an awful mess
but it's done and that's par for the course at my age, pet.
I never wore a cap and I lost my hair too young.
Your head is not a golf course to be shorn.
I can't take those holes in my stride and hope
your GP remembers the best iron to go the distance
the right tee for liveliness the driver to get past
the rough and hazards and not to hack up the fairway
on tryouts. Cancers root deepdownward –
they don't always splay like blooms.
You don't need to tell me how despair spreads
or doesn't. It hugged my vertebrae and held on
until the back branched once and I'm still here
to know too well how exposure works its way indoors.

We need to talk about your shoulders. I only see them
when you sit down, which ought to be more often.
Could they pass as a Jackson Pollock installation?
It'd pay for a skin graft, no shadow of a doubt.
I don't believe you'd joke. I'll book a consultation tomorrow.
Would you rather my skin be blank, dote? Unwritten?
I wouldn't want Henry Cotton for your physician,
plucking out the bacteria-heavy parts of your being

like so much stuffing as if a father could be reverse-
taxidermied. But there's no harm in additional opinions.
It's reckless to place your life in the hands of any old medic.
I don't give a damn for cutting-edge tactic
gentle manner or knowledge of your history.
Heartbreak too, darling, is hard to see from the outside.

We need to talk about your doctor. There was word
he barely takes precautions. He glances over your skin
as if it was cling film masking any old organism.
But if it was, you would keep for longer.
You might keep forever.

Caoilinn Hughes

Were you a strange child with a taste for verse? When I was nine, Yeats was
my bespectacled hero. Dylan Thomas and Yevtushenko were my bag
at ten. By twelve, I'd added Heaney, Whitman, Larkin, Bishop, Boland,
Muldoon, Plath, Kennelly, Frost, Beckett, Neruda and Shakespeare to the
mix the way I added Baileys, Cava, Guinness, Peach Schnapps, Vodka
and Vino Tinto to the pint glass that I was. Novels were for lightweights
who needed mixer.

(More truthfully, I found novels intimidating. Whereas poems were
small, like me, and, admittedly, dense).

Who is your favourite character in a poem? Lady Lazarus. But I'm not sure
you'd invite her round for dinner.

Someone offers you €1,000,000 to never write again: What is your response?
Pound-of-flesh my way around it.

*It's the centenary of the Easter Rising: does this fact matter to you and if so,
in what way?* I was teaching Yeats's 'Easter 1916' this January to a very
diverse group of students, most of whom weren't au fait with the history.
But once I'd done my bit, and we read the poem together, it felt... like
something. Like Carver's bub drawing the cathedral. Something right,
moving, and even (write it!) vital. This will be a year of remembering
Irish history; reassessing our cultural and social standing in light of what's
changed, and, indeed, what hasn't.

If someone described you as a political poet, what would your reaction be? Sure,
yes. Sometimes. I've written poems concerned with bio-ethics, and others
looking at social politics. I'm living in the Netherlands at the moment, so
I'm aware that it's not representative of the real world. It's the most progressive society I've ever spent time in (in terms of how public services
function. They're not necessarily progressive all round... I'm troubled by
the heavily streamed school system, for example, and have you heard of
Zwarte Piet??). There are silent carriages on the train, which is surely the
measure of a people's civility. Can you imagine asking a pack of Dublin
lads to zip it for the duration of their Luas journey? A middle-aged man
recently helped me to build up the courage to scold a group of seven-foot
businessmen sitting opposite for talking on their phones. And it worked!
No one cursed. No one blushed. The eyebrows didn't even stay lifted
for long. It was a *reasonable* request. (Albeit another time, I was told:
'The world's not all about you, lady. I'm not turning down my music.

You move if you want everything your way'). Of course, the lack of guns helps. I find these instances thrilling and threatening: how we treat one another individually and collectively when we are *out in the world*, doing our amateur policing of self and other. There was an electric charge behind this question in Ireland in 2009. How honest can we get now, about ourselves? Do we really want to be responsible? So many things only work if we agree to make them work together: the classroom, cycling lanes, Uber, picking out broken glass from the sand, shard by shard, not making physical contact with strangers without consent, not staring, cultivating an environment of constructive thoughtful criticism, resisting the impulse towards aggression even when there's cause for anger, understanding that public masturbation is not cool. That's all politics, I think. These sorts of thing occupy my thoughts, too much for sound mental health, probably.

What's your worst poetry habit? Not writing it. I spend far far too much time putting off starting new poems because I don't think I can do it. (Most of the time, I can't). I also have a fiction habit, which gets in the way.

You've arranged a date for 8pm, but it's 8.10pm now. You're working on a poem and it's going well. What do you do? I was two-and-a-half hours late for my first date with my partner. And that was just because I was at the end of a good book. If I was in the middle of a good poem, I wouldn't even be capable of texting to cancel the date, for fear of losing the poem. The statistics for finding another date are favourable. Whereas, as Langston Hughes put it, 'poems are like rainbows: they escape you quickly.' Don't look away if you see one.

Have you ever used a poem to seduce someone? If so, what poem was it? (And did it work?) I spent my single youth declaring my (unrequited) love for people, in borrowed verse. I won't mention which poems I used, because most of the time (and actually really once) it resulted in terrified boys hiding behind curtains. So it wouldn't be fair to the poems. But now that I'm in a requited-love scenario, I can name poems without slandering the poet. I recently recited Alan Gillis' 'In Whose Blent Air All Our Compulsions Meet', #7, and why would anyone hide behind a curtain at that? 'I want to do with you / what darkness does with candlelight'!

Who will play the poet in the Hollywood adaptation of your last poem? Michael Fassbender, in my dreams. James Franco, in my nightmares.

You're invited to read in a major festival: what are your top three backstage demands? No cameras. No dogs. No, I don't care that he's harmless.

What's your current favourite word? Puny.

Would you rather win the TS Eliot Prize or the Prize Bonds? Where's the poet's name in Prize Bonds? Eliot all the way.

Cyril Connolly said the true function of a writer is to write a masterpiece, and no other task is of any consequence. Do you agree? Yes, in terms of career/ writing stuff. Absolutely. However, in life, there are other things of consequence, thankfully. Otherwise, all books would be about writing, and that would be dire.

'The hard part is getting to the top of page 1' – Tom Stoppard. What, for you, is the hard part? For poetry, the first lines (getting started). For fiction, I love the start and hate the middle. But I'm pretty sure I'm doing something wrong. I find it all ridiculously hard.

If your ideal poem were an outfit, what would it look like? An assortment of fabrics (that don't go together like tweed, silk, denim and lycra), layers, mutely clashing colours. Not drawing much attention to itself, but interesting, if one chose to pay attention to it. I should say here that when a straight male friend once picked me up from my flat so we could walk to university together, he asked me to go back inside and change. I said I was comfy and I didn't want to be late for the intro to Dada. He said it looked like I'd already been introduced.

What advice would you give to older poets? Consider if you really ought to be writing reviews (different to blurbs, mind you) of poetry books published by *your* publisher. Poetry imprints tend to be small. As such, I don't think it's really honest for poets to review fellow-imprint poets, because of course we want the best for our publishers. That's me being serious. Me being daft: Drop me a line!

Andrew Jamison

WORDS FOR SUMMER

I've wondered if there are words for it,
the end of August, all this loving you.
Blackberries at Burrington, the sea at Brean,
a half of something local at The Plough,
in its garden in the sun in the heat,
or trying to learn to dance, where to stand,
how not to grip your hands too tightly in the hold,
the right amount of tension in the arms.

I've wondered if there will be words for it
again, now summer's over, and life,
the working world, with timetables and terms,
is calling our names in its register
to which we must respond with 'here' or 'present'
even if we're not, thinking only
of garden and picked fruit, The Plough and the sea,
of hands and of arms and of holding.

Andrew Jamison

THE NIGHT YOU BECAME A COUNTY

Not even a week away and it's been tough
to see a thing as a thing in itself
without seeing something of you. Take The Mournes
visible from a Killyleagh hill,
how their undulations took on your skin and bones,
each Slieve contouring into the next, anatomical;
your shoulder seemed so much like Donard,
your neck The Devil's Bite, your elbow Binnian.
And what was the water, Strangford Lough itself,
but your language, your words, your speaking voice,
not your whistling or your song – too good –
but your plain speech, telling me things:
words I wanted to hear, and words that were true.
Your accent went forgotten
until there was sight of the shoreline drawing
away to the north; and your breath, your breath,
your breath was the water of where I'm from.

Andrew Jamison

Were you a strange child with a taste for verse? I don't remember having a taste for verse as a child, or in fact reading much at all. I do remember being outside a lot, though, being fairly happy in my own company, wandering around the fields, or kicking a ball about with my brothers. I do remember, however, 'the coal / Glittering in its shed'.

Do you too dislike it? It's a cynical world, and one of the challenges I find is constantly reminding myself what it is I love about poetry. For me it comes down to how poetry opens up the life we live beneath the life we're living, the world that inhabits us. It has to sound good, too. So, no, I love it really.

Who is your favourite character in a poem? Colmcille, in the ancient Irish poem, translated by John Montague, is a figure that I keep returning to. While I can't relate to being an 'exile' in the proper sense of that word, I, like many others, I'd guess, can relate to the sense of wanting to go back to where I'm from. I live and work in England, but in many ways I've never left Northern Ireland. It's a poem about how the imagination enables us to inhabit an elsewhere, and how that elsewhere can sustain us.

Have you ever glued pages of a poetry book together? I wouldn't waste the glue.

It's the centenary of the Easter Rising: does this fact matter to you and if so, in what way? I feel like I should have more to say about the Easter Rising. Being brought up in a Protestant Northern Ireland, I can't say it was something I was taught much about in school, but that's no excuse. It matters to me in the way that all violent loss of life matters to me, in the way that all atrocities involving innocent civilians matter to me, which is to say a lot, which is also to say it should matter to me a great deal more.

If you could pick a time to be dropped amongst the three best poets alive at that moment, when would it be and who would they be? I'm currently teaching *Paradise Lost*, and, with it, realising for the first time the importance of the seventeenth century for poetry. It seems to me to be a time when poetry had found a new lease of life and had a real, urgent purpose. It's interesting to think that when Milton was labouring over an epic like *Paradise Lost*, Basho was working on haiku, and Jonathan Swift, though a bit later on, was getting satirical in Dublin. It seems like an amazingly innovative time, when the art was being pushed and pulled in many different directions. I'm not really sure we do live in a golden age of poetry, and I think we'll be waiting a long while before another Heaney-like genius comes along. It was great to have been alive while he was here and writing, though.

What's your worst poetry habit? In my heart of hearts, I'm not one of the great innovators of poetry, in fact I've only got about two poems: couplets (rhymed or unrhymed) and blank verse. My poetry is not immune to the contemporary disease of the imperative either.

Have you ever carried a poem by someone else around on your person? If so, what was it? I can't say I've ever carried a single poem, but I used to carry Louis MacNeice's *Selected Poems* (edited by Michael Longley) around with me a lot as an undergraduate. 'Meeting Point' with its incantatory repetition was the first poem to really make me sit up and listen to the language. *101 Sonnets*, edited by Don Paterson, which is currently in my schoolbag, always yields a surprise, and usually that surprise is how one rigid form of poetry can be so malleable, and susceptible to innovation.

What's your current favourite word? Autocthonous is a good one. But I'd have to say *Aereopagitica*, the title of Milton's pamphlet defending free speech, which, ironically, I struggle to pronounce, much to the amusement of my students.

Would you rather win the TS Eliot Prize or the Prize Bonds? I think I remember winning about £50 in the Bonds when I was young, and that felt pretty good. As for poetry prizes, time is the best judge of the poems and the poet.

Let's assume you're 60 and still publishing poems: what do you want to have achieved between now and then? To continue to love the language, to continue to be surprised by it, to continue to see others writing great poetry, to have continued.

Cyril Connolly said the true function of a writer is to write a masterpiece, and no other task is of any consequence. Do you agree? I can't say I've ever really thought about writing a masterpiece, getting around to the next line is mostly hard enough. This is all I know about the function of a writer: sometimes you write a poem, sometimes you don't. Sometimes it gets published, sometimes it doesn't. Sometimes someone likes it, sometimes they don't.

'The hard part is getting to the top of page 1' – Tom Stoppard. What, for you, is the hard part? The hard part, for me, especially during the school term, is getting to the desk. When I'm there, the hard part is putting my laptop

away and not getting distracted by the internet. When I've done that, the writing weirdly takes care of itself; the whole process of writing a poem has always been a bit of a blur for me and I'm never entirely sure how it happens. Then comes the Penrose Stairs of the editing process.

What advice would you give to older poets? 'Keep at it.' I don't think anyone is too old for encouragement when it comes to writing, which is also to say that I don't think anyone outgrows the self-doubt and insecurity inherent in attempting to write.

Is there any question you wish you'd been asked here (that you'd like to answer now?) As an English teacher in a secondary school, who is your favourite poet to teach?

I got the opportunity to teach 'The Waste Land' a year or two ago, which was daunting at first (how do you *teach* a poem like that?) but, once you let go of it and let the students come to terms with the language as a music in itself, it's powerful stuff. I love teaching Seamus Heaney, though. As well as writing poems that are at once clear and rich, he was also a wonderful spokesperson for poetry, and someone who talked so eloquently and unfussily about the business of writing, in a way that pretty much everyone from eleven upwards can understand. I can't think of anybody else, alive or dead, who as well as being a great writer, was also so brilliant at speaking about their writing, and the writing of others. One of the many things poetry will miss about Heaney is his ability to translate the act of it in human terms.

Victoria Kennefick

CORK SCHOOLGIRL CONSIDERS THE GPO O'CONNELL STREET, DUBLIN 2016

I am sixteen, standing outside the GPO
in my school uniform, which isn't ideal.

My uniform is the colour of bull's blood.

I am sixteen, a pleasing symmetry because
I love history, have I told you that?

It is mine so I carry it in my rucksack.

I love all the men of history sacrificing
themselves for Ireland, for me, like rebel Jesuses.

I put my finger in the building's bullet holes;

poke around in its wounds.
I wonder if they feel it,

those boys, younger than me,

I hope they do, their blooming faces
pressed flat in the pages of my books.

I lick the wall as if it were a stamp,

it tastes of bones, this smelly city,
of those boys in uniforms,

theirs bloody too. I put my lips

to the pillar. I want to kiss them all. And
I do, I kiss all those boys goodbye.

Victoria Kennefick

THE TALK

when I asked what the word meant
I was directed to the dictionary.
My older half-sister showed me
the entry, her grave thumb covered
all the interesting bits

when she climbed a tree in our front garden
my best friend's knickers flashed,
the gusset soiled rust-red; I said nothing
but she didn't come out to play
for five whole days

when our science teacher told us to open
the pinkest chapter, all I could think of was
Michelangelo's *David* but Mr Kelly keeled over
on the wooden stool, his forehead
kissing bare plastic tile

when a young man, older than me
in double-denim, sucked the alcopop
tongue out of my head,
shoved his hands under the clefts
of my bottom

I figured it out.

Victoria Kennefick

Were you a strange child with a taste for verse? In truth, every child I've ever known has been strange in some glorious way. It isn't something that vanishes either, we just become more adept at camouflage. My taste for verse was my particular peculiarity. I collected weird, silly and rude words as other children might collect stamps, or rocks, or football cards. I enjoyed playing with them too, and watching the reaction my use of them would elicit from the adults in my life – shock or pride. I was an anxious child, what adults euphemistically refer to as 'sensitive' (alas, I think this often, and still, has negative connotations). Reading verse was extremely helpful to me in this regard, reciting poems I had learned off by heart calmed my nerves. Poetry made sense to me, puns cracked me up. I was very lucky to be encouraged in this strangeness by my parents, my family and by my teachers – though as a result I wasn't the most popular kid in the class by a long shot, as you can well imagine.

Who is your favourite character in a poem? I have a number of favourite characters in poems; of course that keeps changing the more I read and discover. At the moment I am a little bit in love with Hulk in Greg Santos' poem 'Hulk Smash!' which is a brilliant, refreshing and delight-ful example of a persona poem. It has an epigraph by Frank O'Hara from 'Meditations in an Emergency' – 'I am the least difficult of men. All I want is boundless love.' For the longest time I have also had a soft spot for Felix Randal in the Gerard Manley Hopkins poem of the same name. He taught me so much about humility. I also fancy J Alfred Prufrock a little bit, which I realise may be problematic. My all-time favourite though is Plath's magnificent and fearsome Lady Lazarus.

If you could die and come back as a poem, what poem would it be? I intend to come back as Emily Dickinson's 'Because I could not stop for Death'.

Someone offers you €1,000,000 to never write again: What is your response? The minuscule area of my brain that is concerned with monetary mat-ters, such as having enough food to eat and a roof over my head is screaming at me, *Take the money and run, girl*. But thankfully it is a very teensy part so I can happily ignore it, and often do to the detriment of my bank balance. Poetry, every time.

It's the centenary of the Easter Rising: does this fact matter to you and if so, in what way? All historical events that have shaped our current society matter, it is vital to examine and to learn from the experiences of the past. I have the utmost respect and gratitude for those that took part in the Ris-ing. I particularly admire the women of the time; their vision for Ireland is one we have yet to live up to. Their participation is worth investigating further, particularly as we still have such a poor record on women's rights in this country. They still have much to teach us.

Would you rather be the poet or the poem? I would much rather be the poem. A brilliant epic book-length one of course.

If you could pick a time to be dropped amongst the three best poets alive at that moment, when would it be? While there are many contenders, I knew the answer to this question immediately. I would put myself in the way of Sylvia Plath, Anne Sexton and George Starbuck when they were students of Robert Lowell at Boston University in the late 1950s. That being said, I think now is an exciting time to be a poet in Ireland. I feel privileged to be between the covers with so many talented Irish poets in this issue of *PIR*.

What's your worst poetry habit? I have all the bad habits when it comes to poetry. I am not going to reveal them here, but at the moment everything is under control. I promise.

You've arranged a date for 8pm, but it's 8.10pm now. You're working on a poem and it's going well. What do you do? In the past, I would have been ridiculously late which would, understandably, incur the wrath of the person I was to meet. I have learned my lesson. Don't make dates, write poetry (I have a very understanding spouse).

Have you ever carried a poem by someone else around on your person? I do carry around poems, and books too. For a time I carried around *Dear Boy* by Emily Berry, which was a breakthrough book for my own writing. At the moment I have 'Ugly' by Warsan Shire in my bag. I also downloaded the Poetry Foundation app on my phone a year or so ago. It's free and brilliant. It has a 'Spin' function which allows you to discover poems on various themes that you mightn't come across otherwise. That's always in my pocket. I also carry around poems I am working on, it can be helpful to have them to hand when a problem resolves or creates itself.

A family member says, 'You should write a poem about that': what do you do? I think particularly of Flannery O'Connor when relatives suggest this to me. She dealt with such unsolicited advice from visitors who suggested she write another *Gone With the Wind* 'like that lady in Atlanta did', referring of course to Margaret Mitchell. O'Connor responded with trademark brilliance in one of her most famous stories, 'A Good Man Is Hard to Find', where the grandmother, a 'good Christian woman', reflects sentimentally on the old order of the South, an order that is now, 'Gone with the Wind'. Like O'Connor did, I imagine, I smile and nod. Only sometimes do I use their suggestion. Though maybe not in the way they envisaged.

Have you ever used a poem to seduce someone? If so, what poem was it? (And did it work?) Of course. I am a poet! I have often used poetry to seduce. I am rather adept at reciting poems drunkenly at parties. Though not so much anymore. I recited ee cummings' 'i carry your heart with me...' on my wedding day. I'm pretty sure that it's this seduction method that ultimately snagged my spouse. Who wouldn't want to be married to a poet?

You're given a choice: either every poem or no poem you write from now on must use the word 'I'. Which do you choose? 'I', 'I' every time. I am in love with the first-person and there is no cure for it.

Who will play the poet in the Hollywood adaptation of your last poem? Tilda Swinton.

You're invited to read at a major festival: what are your top three backstage demands? Smelling salts, altitude sickness medication, a black cashmere cape, decaf coffee (from a machine) and a pomegranate. I know that's more than three, but I don't play by the rules.

What's your current favourite word? Fizz, Rebel and Questionnaire.

If your ideal poem were an outfit, what would it look like? See black cashmere cape above, combined with fitted white silk shirt, leather trousers and pointed black patent ankle boots with gold buckles. This poem's nails would be painted plum with lipstick to match. Around its neck, a long thin gold chain with a tooth dangling from it, and encrusted in this tooth, a perfectly tear-shaped ruby.

What advice would you give older poets? I am extremely grateful to older poets. I am in no position to offer them advice. Rather I would ask advice of them, possibly whilst pressing my pamphlet into their hands, whisper-ing *Please read this*, followed by a barely audible but emphatic, *Help me*. Every poet needs a mentor.

Is there any question you wish you'd been asked here (that you'd like to answer now?) Would you accept this generous cheque as an advance for your first poetry collection?

Marcus Mac Conghail

AN TEIRIPEOIR

D'iompraíos mo cheann go dochtúir na gceann
i mála plaisteach
(amach as an nósreoiteoir a thógas é)
seomra an dochtúra
seomra nach raibh seanchaite
ná nuadhaite
seomra nár thug faic le fios
is thosnaíos ag cur síos
ar mo cheann
é suite ansan ar an mbord
eadrainn.

D'aithin sí nithe, mhol sí, luaigh is threoraigh
is nuair a d'éiríos chun an ciarsúr
a thug sí dom
a chaitheamh isteach sa bhin
anuas ar chiarsúir eile a thit sé
is nuair a chasas le filleadh
ar mo shuíochán
bhí slabhra de bhlaoscanna
crochta ón tsíleáil
agus mise suite romham
ar aghaidh an dochtúra amach,
ag déanamh cur i láthair.

Marcus Mac Conghail

TOCHT

Níl dromchla na leapan
déanta de leath má leath
is níl lár na leapan
suite sa lár go baileach.

Seilbh, glactar
is géilltear talamh
gach re seal –
scáildhráma na beatha
ar an mbraillín bhán.

Marcus Mac Conghail

Were you a strange child with a taste for verse? Ní rabhas ait agus mé im leanbh agus ní raibh luí agam le véarsaíocht. Ach is leanbh ait anois mé agus luím le véarsaíocht.

Do you too dislike it? #dearfach

Who is your favourite character in a poem? Pound sa dán 'Do Phound, ó Dhia' le Michael Davitt.

If you could die and come back as a poem, what poem would it be? 'An Odaisé' – an t-aistriúchán iontach a dhein Pádraig de Brún.

Someone offers you €1,000,000 to never write again: What is your response? Thógfainn an t-airgead agus scríobhfainn seiceanna fileata.

Have you ever glued pages of a poetry book together? Stop dorais – d'úsáideas leabhar mar stop dorais. Níor bhain mé triail as an ngliú rud fós.

It's the centenary of the Easter Rising: does this fact matter to you and if so, in what way? Faighim €40 as é seo a scríobh agus braithim gur ag útamáil atáim sa scipéad smeartha.

If someone described you as a political poet, what would your reaction be? Thuigfinn nach raibh Gaeilge ag an duine sin, nó, thuigfinn go raibh Gaeilge ag an duine sin, nó, thuigfinn nach raibh mo chuid dánta léite ag an duine sin, nó thuigfinn go raibh mo chuid dánta léite ag an duine sin.

Would you rather be the poet or the poem? B'fhearr liom bheith im dhán – tá ord, slacht, soiléireacht agus críochnúlacht i gceist le dán.

If you could pick a time to be dropped amongst the three best poets alive at that moment, when would it be and who would they be? Tábhairne Sheáin Uí Thuama i gCromadh, Luimneach 1735 – ag cúléisteacht le Seán, Aindrias Mac Craith agus Seán Clárach Mac Domhnaill agus iad ag sárú a chéile.

What's your worst poetry habit? Na dánta nach gcríochnaím. Na dánta nach dtosnaím. Na dánta nach ritheann liom.

You've arranged a date for 8pm, but it's 8.10pm now. You're working on a poem and it's going well. What do you do? Toitín a dheargadh.

Have you ever carried a poem by someone else around on your person? If so, what was it? Nuair a bhí glicghuthán agam bhíodh gach dán le gach duine im phóca agam an t-am go léir.

A family member says, 'You should write a poem about that': what do you do? Bhuel, dála gach coimisiún, chinnteoinn méid na híocaíochta ar dtús.

If your best poem were a weekend away, where would it be? Ar an tear i mBarcelona.

It's a good poem but it's forty-one lines long and the competition with the big prize specifies a max of forty: what do you do? D'úsáidfainn an chéad líne don teideal.

Have you ever used a poem to seduce someone? If so, what poem was it? (And did it work?) Is suiríocht é gach dán – féin-suiríocht, ag suirí leis an lucht éisteachta/léite, agus uaireanta le duine ar leith a mhealladh. Táim ciontach.

You're given a choice: either every poem or no poem you write from now on must use the word 'I'. Which do you choose? Ní nós liom 'I' a úsáid – ach táim tugtha don táite :)

Your friend is depressed: what's the very last poetry book you'd give him/her? Níl tuairim agam.

Who will play the poet in the Hollywood adaptation of your last poem? Is francach (le f beag) a scríobh an dán is déanaí a chríochnaigh mé. Só, ag brath ar an athchóiriú, Scabbers, peata Ron Weasley, nó an francach a bhí i seomra 101 sa scannán a déanadh de 1984.

You're invited to read in a major festival: what are your top three backstage demands? Iad seo a bheith ar stáitse – Drumadóir. Dordaire. Giotáraí.

What's your current favourite word? Gáiriteach.

You're proud of the poem but know it will offend someone you don't even like: what do you do? Is deacair a rá. Inis an fhírinne agus ná gortaigh daoine? – ach sin dhá rud nach ndéanaim.

Would you rather win the TS Eliot Prize or the Prize Bonds? B'fhearr liomsa duais Oireachtais a bhuachaint.

Let's assume you're 60 and still publishing poems: what do you want to have achieved between now and then? Go mbeinn tar éis triail a bhaint as guthanna éagsúla.

Cyril Connolly said the true function of a writer is to write a masterpiece, and no other task is of any consequence. Do you agree? Níl tuairim agam.

'The hard part is getting to the top of page 1' – Tom Stoppard. What, for you, is the hard part? An rud is deacra domsa ná dán a scríobh gan foclóir.

If your ideal poem were an outfit, what would it look like? Huggy Bear.

What advice would you give to older poets? Lean oraibh ag taispeáint na slí.

Is there any question you wish you'd been asked here (that you'd like to answer now?) An scríbhneoir éadmhar tú? – Sea, gach uair a léim líne mhaith le scríbhneoir eile ceannaím arsanaic.

Robert Herbert McClean

from RIFFAGE BEASTINGS

III

this evening the porno and the hotline /
bling edgy / so so / this dusk is damage
proof and i'm a filthy fucking animal /
in clearings gun toting girl gangs take
pot shots at what's left of the stars / put windows
out with untrained aim / bullets whiz through pink
fog / take leaves from trees / petals from flowers /
they tried to make me go to rehab but
i was all like no no no i'm lonely
you can shut up and you can shut up
too / you're not going to compare me
to the actual pollution / bitch be
all like back and forth talking such slang whip /

VII

on the verge of participating
rein it in / crash diet for a wedding
at which you rush the dancefloor because
the dj dropped dead in silence and shadow /
midnight and pissed up / orgy with the bridesmaids /
shona and oonagh and niamh and orla /
testosterone for every one and drinks
to toast the hot wager and slip on a sheath /
oonagh and shona and orla and niamh /
their names a comfort to my throat and eyes /
i toyed like a time bomb / it was super
fun / actually super fucking heaven /
deep heaven / clear heaven vantage point / yeah
that mirror ball is exactly the problem

X

leather swivel/ mooch mooch/ time share lease/ fail safe
psychotherapist/ fail safe sum/ won't even
be dust in the all ever after/ feels
like a matrix in a matrix something
that could've been on tv once like i in
an advert for the kindling fire that brought
this all about for christ's sake/ magenta
flashes made the sky metal solid like
a lid to clang and those of us left to
bruise and bloat and float to the metal lid
and our heads about it like gun shots to
windows we dream/ we dream into and through this
lid/ liquid now like silk on the ocean span
and we awake dull dreamers/ chat shades/

Robert Herbert McClean

Were you a strange child with a taste for verse? When I was maybe five or six my parents told me to write my letter to Santa Claus, much to the amusement of my two teenage sisters. When I wrote down what I wanted for Christmas, I couldn't bear my embarrassment. I hid behind the sofa. Of course, two teenage sisters goading in the moment relieved me of my letter and read it aloud to my parents. I'd asked Santa Claus for Linda Lusardi. My dad would often read me the Lord's Prayer.

Do you too dislike it? Yes. I too dislike that the richest 1% is set to overtake the other 99% of the world's population in terms of wealth. I too dislike that 1 in 9 people on this planet do not have enough to eat on a daily basis and that more than a billion people still live on less than $1.25 per day. I too dislike that we bailed out the banks, that free healthcare and education is not a human right the world over. I too dislike that we still have to endure gender inequality, racism and homophobia. I too dislike that the monotony and ignorance projected and perpetuated by mainstream popular culture dulls our potential for social revolution. Welcome to the Anthropocene. Dry your eyes.

Who is your favourite character in a poem? Mr Bones.

If you could die and come back as a poem, what poem would it be? My obituary.

Someone offers you €1,000,000 to never write again: What is your response? What is the current exchange rate to sterling? Can we negotiate the terms and conditions?

Have you ever glued pages of a poetry book together? Worse. I became a poet.

It's the centenary of the Easter Rising: does this fact matter to you and if so, in what way? I was born into a mixed marriage in the North of Ireland. I wasn't always encouraged to express a political opinion during the Troubles, or post-conflict. I was brought up to challenge adversity and sectarianism. It was extremely important to me that both Irish Catholics and Protestants led that rebellion together. Imperialism bad. Revolution good.

If someone described you as a political poet, what would your reaction be? Aye. And what?

Would you rather be the poet or the poem? The poet is the poem. Chicken and egg. Cart before the horse. Quantum physics.

If you could pick a time to be dropped amongst the three best poets alive at that moment, when would it be and who would they be? It would probably be the early twentieth century and the poets would be Mina Loy, Blaise Cendrars and me. If you don't believe in yourself you can't expect anyone else to. We should all feel entitled, empowered and brave enough to pursue our dreams.

What's your worst poetry habit? Sure that's what poetry is. Is this a trick question?

You've arranged a date for 8pm, but it's 8.10pm now. You're working on a poem and it's going well. What do you do? Ring the person you're meeting and apologise, because unless you live within five minutes of the place at which you've agreed to meet, you've been selfish and rude. People before poems.

Have you ever carried a poem by someone else around on your person? If so, what was it? I sometimes think about a Dennis Cooper poem which impressed me greatly about a cottaging sailor.

A family member says, 'You should write a poem about that': what do you do? Think: that is so nice of you to engage with this marginal art I practice, you show empathy. I love you. That was such a nice gesture, I'm very lucky to have this considerate and encouraging family to belong to.

If your best poem were a weekend away, where would it be? Somewhere I've never been.

It's a good poem but it's forty-one lines long and the competition with the big prize specifies a max of forty: what do you do? Call in some favours.

Have you ever used a poem to seduce someone? If so, what poem was it? (And did it work?) I'm currently reading the collected poems of Bataille.

You're given a choice: either every poem or no poem you write from now on must use the word 'I'. Which do you choose? I choose no future poem to use the word 'I'. This semantic deviation will be the saviour of humanity.

Your friend is depressed: what's the very last poetry book you'd give him/her? Is this question designed to make me a critic? I'd be a better friend and see if they want to talk it out.

Who will play the poet in the Hollywood adaptation of your last poem? With minimum preparation and natural talent, me.

You're invited to read in a major festival: what are your top three backstage demands? I don't like to make demands of people. I think that's vulgar.

What's your current favourite word? Payment.

You're proud of the poem but know it will offend someone you don't even like: what do you do? Offence like all things is relative. Pride should be earned on serious reflection and be balanced by good intention and humility.

Would you rather win the TS Eliot Prize or the Prize Bonds? It might be a statement if I won the TS Eliot prize and refused to accept it, but I'd like to win it and to accept it. If I was to refuse the prize bond winnings I think I'd be known as an idiot.

Let's assume you're 60 and still publishing poems: what do you want to have achieved between now and then? Generally, to have been the best compassionate and patient version of myself to all my friends and family. Specifically, to have written, directed and scored a feature film.

Cyril Connolly said the true function of a writer is to write a masterpiece, and no other task is of any consequence. Do you agree? Whether I feed my cat and give her fresh water is of consequence. So I think Cyril was talking some highfalutin romanticism. That said, if you're going to do something, do it right.

'The hard part is getting to the top of page 1' – Tom Stoppard. What, for you, is the hard part? Thinking about Tom Stoppard. If writing was easy what would be the point?

If your ideal poem were an outfit, what would it look like? There wouldn't be an outfit. There wouldn't be need for an outfit.

What advice would you give to older poets? Don't go on the ego trip fuelled by the death drive. Don't compromise. Be your own critic. Believe.

Is there any question you wish you'd been asked here (that you'd like to answer now?) What advice would you give to younger poets? Don't go on the ego trip fuelled by the death drive. Don't compromise. Be your own critic. Believe.

Afric McGlinchey

THE ATTIC AND THE ID

No stair to take me there, just a drop-down ladder
that vanishes after my vanishing feet; a spider abseils
a single thread among the dust motes to a landing strip,
with chitins that intuit when to cling and when release.
No supper tonight; I'm dining on silence and other
senses while I journey along my own silk road.
No inclination for bed. I sleep poorly anyway,
and here is respite from the pressure even to try.
Instead, I'm dipping into your African story.

You dispensed with socks and sense, took to night
spots and hookers, gambled away all your belongings
in twenty minutes. I compare my small life
with your adventures, and back I go, to our foray
into those African clubs, where slim-hipped girls
crossed legs seductively, flashing thigh and crotch,
and stared at you, the only white man. The city sparkled.
You took my hand, startled the floor with moves
you learned from mambas and black rhythm;

this reminding me of last night's reggae in De Barra's,
decades falling away, and the wall he pushed me up
against to kiss me, starting a thrill I haven't
felt in years, that was just as quickly quenched
when he spied his ex and desisted. And oh!
I miss your nonchalance, forbidden glance that
left me in no doubt and leaves me wanting, still.
Pulse is in the mind more than the body; I find
that I touch strangers more easily than family.

Let me return to the memory of that surprise
kiss, and perhaps another if the glass is full
and lights are low. He wants me younger, too,
a man-thing, primed to want the taut and thin –
and I disappoint; but can swerve his thoughts
to lust with the erotica of words. From you,
and this spider, I learn the language
of a web, feel ready now to leave the attic;
drop down, to complete my weaving.

Afric McGlinchey

BACK TO SALT

The crush of the crowd slackens
as I walk away, its roar still in my ears.
How I hate this city, wrapped
in smog, so far from the shale
cliffs of my childhood.

New days would arrive
delicately; a silk sky, wavering.
I'd throw my voice into blowholes
filling and emptying; search
below water for secrets.

Now this other life, like a second
pillow too bulky to sleep with.
I move along streets,
their grime-defined corners
needling, scraping.

Next thing I'll be turning
into a coffeehouse addict,
marmalade breakfasts
in the afternoon,
windows offering a reminder

of life, while I absorb e-news.
I let the sounds percolate in:
waves echoing through
miles of memory
and light, untangling time.

Afric McGlinchey

Were you a strange child with a taste for verse? A bit odd, I suppose! Always up a tree with a book. We moved a lot. Books were my anchor. I heard nothing of the bombs going off all around me.

Do you too dislike it? Oh yes – but once you have discovered a genuine poem like Mark Doty's 'A Green Crab's Shell', well, you keep reading, hoping for more like that. And you want to – you WANT to – write poetry that can do something similar for a reader.

Who is your favourite character in a poem? Prufrock. I completely identify with his tentativeness, doubt, yearning.

If you could die and come back as a poem, what poem would it be? For today, I'll opt for 'The Listeners', by Walter de la Mare. A poem I recited so often to my children that they knew it by heart at the ages of five and seven. A question I keep asking myself: 'Is there anybody there…?'

Someone offers you €1,000,000 never to write again: What is your response? Well, I can't not write, so that wouldn't work! No amount of money would.

Have you ever glued pages of a poetry book together? Er, no. But I have made marks in them. Disparaging remarks too. Like, 'aarrghhh!!!!'

It's the centenary of the Easter Rising: does this fact matter to you and if so, in what way? It's interesting, in terms of how the Rising impacted on personal lives. I'm currently judging the Poets Meet Politics competition, and reading a number of such poems.

If someone described you as a political poet, what would your reaction be? Somehow, being identified as a political poet can sound as dismissive as being called a confessional poet. That's the danger of labels. They're too confining. Although to be called a lyric poet would be bearable!

Would you rather be the poet or the poem? I would like to be the poet with the poem! The delivery of a poem can help it transcend to a different level. Billy Ramsell, Alice Oswald and Paul Durcan all have this gift.

If you could pick a time to be dropped amongst the three best poets alive at that moment, when would it be and who would they be? So many possibilities, eras, countries! Maybe Dylan Thomas, Rosemary Tonks and Sylvia Plath – at the point where all three were living! All of their influences inspire me too;

so I'd get to stand on the shoulders of those standing on the shoulders of giants...

What's your worst poetry habit? Sending out work prematurely.

You've arranged a date for 8pm, but it's 8.10pm now. You're working on a poem and it's going well. What do you do? Text an apology, get the bones of it down, then, while driving to the date, if ideas/lines are still coming, record them on audio.

Have you ever carried a poem by someone else around on your person? If so, what was it? Actually, just recently I did that with the winner of the Ballymaloe competition. It was 'My Blue Hen' by Ann Gray, a beautiful poem. But usually, I'll carry around whatever collection I'm reading: currently, it's Anne Carson's *Red Doc>*.

A family member says, 'You should write a poem about that': what do you do? I bear it in mind, but unless the poem comes spontaneously, I won't write it.

If your best poem were a weekend away, where would it be? It would be somewhere I've never been. Perhaps Havana. Or Iceland.

It's a good poem but it's forty-one lines long and the competition with the big prize specifies a max of forty: what do you do? Rearrange the lines. Or edit a little more, so that the poem naturally loses a line.

Have you ever used a poem to seduce someone? If so, what poem was it? (And did it work?) One by someone else? No. One by me – not to seduce someone, but to keep him from leaving: 'Hold On', which is in my debut collection. (And yes, it did).

You're given a choice: either every poem or no poem you write from now on must use the word 'I'. Which do you choose? Well, I do gravitate to 'I' poems, both by others and in my own work, as you can see from the poems in this issue! So no contest really. But I'd try to develop the habit of delaying the 'I' word until as late as possible in the poem.

Your friend is depressed: what's the very last poetry book you'd give him/her? Kobus Moolman's *A Book of Rooms*. Although, on second thoughts, it might be the perfect book!

Who will play the poet in the Hollywood adaptation of your last poem? Ha. Juliette Binoche. That's Hollywood. Fantasy!

You're invited to read in a major festival: what are your top three backstage demands? Sparkling water with a slice of lemon. A basin to brush my teeth. Privacy.

What's your current favourite word? Pareidolia.

You're proud of the poem but know it will offend someone you don't even like: what do you do? I'll cross my fingers they don't see it. (Although I did go so far as to delete two poems in reprints of my first collection, in case they were spotted).

Would you rather win the TS Eliot Prize or the Prize Bonds? TS Eliot. Rolls so nicely off the tongue…

Let's assume you're 60 and still publishing poems: what do you want to have achieved between now and then? A long, formal poem. Invitations to festivals in Colombia and Iceland. Another collection or two. A big award!

Cyril Connolly said the true function of a writer is to write a masterpiece, and no other task is of any consequence. Do you agree? It's the dream! In the meantime, hopefully, you keep raising the bar for yourself. Until one day, maybe you're divinely inspired, and it happens…

'The hard part is getting to the top of page 1' – Tom Stoppard. What, for you, is the hard part? Murdering the little darlings. Although I'm getting more bloodthirsty.

If your ideal poem were an outfit, what would it look like? A forties trench coat, with the collar up, and a fedora or Ingrid Bergman's *Casablanca* hat so there's only the briefest glimpse of a profile in the shadows.

What advice would you give to older poets? Invent a persona of a different gender and decade, who gives advice to older poets.

Is there any question you wish you'd been asked here (that you'd like to answer now?) Yes: Paul Muldoon advises his students to identify their territory – what would you define as your territory?

I think of myself as a nomad, in terms of issues or themes. Unless it's connection; our inter-connectedness. And you can explore that in so many ways. Mark Doty says if you keep doing the same thing, you're not going to get the same depth charge. So, it's about reinventing yourself, trying on different hats. I like the idea of wearing a beret today, a fedora tomorrow.

Jim Maguire

THE ORIENT SINGS TO ELLIE MACSWINEY

Paris, 1870

Feeling the pull of a chord that resists
is more than desire, a craving to live
unfettered by high collars, barrettes.

It's not about playing the elusive
heroine, the one whose sleepwalking scene
reels them in with the glassy impassive

calm she keeps as the effects machine
blows wind through her hair. It's more like falling
through floor after floor of a house she dreams

is flushing itself of everything
that doesn't belong; opening her eyes
to an inscrutable light, a mountain

embroidered on a folding screen, cries
from across the persimmon field of the boy
vendor who heaps the crates so frighteningly high

on his A-frame, echoes of the night soil
man with the doleful chant. All the buried lives
rising, seeping into her voice

from their underground streams. She keeps an eye
out for moist patches where a foot might sink,
sudden scraggy flowers, gorgeous fungi –

signs our lives are not what we think.

Note: *Although she is mainly remembered as 'the devoted Irish wife' of the neurasthenic composer Henri Duparc, after she first came to Paris Ellie MacSwiney (1845-1934) enjoyed a brief career as a soprano. The poem is inspired by a photograph of MacSwiney dressed in a kimono.*

Jim Maguire

ANGELS

I have found intimacy
in unexpected places.
The farrowing box, the trough
on a haze-held morning.
I understand attraction
is never purely physical
for creatures like us
with our propensity for Greek
idealisation; whose fears
are fanned by soughs
in the undergrowth, buckets
of hammed-up obloquies.
Yet for us it is easier to believe
in angels than in gods.
And we know what we believe
doesn't matter half as much
as how we abide
when we're up with our chins
on the rump. Spiky spines
that will prick ever-after
in solitary pens.
Pressed against the vent
of the co-op truck
the sudden kick in the gut.

Jim Maguire

Were you a strange child with a taste for verse? I came to poetry through music. I lived for the annual opera festival in Wexford, where I'm from. A walk-on part in one of the operas led to an unlikely career as a boy soprano. It started with the female lead in *Finian's Rainbow* at St Peter's and ended in Paris with a recording of Miles in *The Turn of the Screw* for Radio France. I also played the piano and, briefly, the cello. I liked how musicians were forced into poetry when they rehearsed, like the conductor telling a singer, 'Don't think of it as soft, think of it as far away...'

Do you too dislike it? The jet fuel of opera at a young age probably had a desensitising effect, but I prefer feeling and intensity over intricacies of meaning. I don't like poems that are too much in the head, especially if they are cautious and smugly ironic, as if they think they can bypass the botheration of feeling. Discussing his work recently, the impressive English poet Andrew McMillan said he was 'not the smartest cookie in the supermarket multipack'. That was refreshing to hear. I file it alongside Les Murray's observation that in poetry 'writers and readers alike ... work beyond our own intelligence'. The worst part of poetry is the fool it makes of me after the poem has been written – the vanity, the pettiness, the way gold turns to tin when the rejection arrives.

Who is your favourite character in a poem? For all his non-appearance in the poem, it's hard to forget Mahon's mycologist from 'A Disused Shed in Co Wexford'. Where did he go? Did he migrate into other poems? Is the 'expropriated' a reference to his move from Agriculture to Finance after the trauma of what happened in the shed? That would explain his night-walking through Kinsella's Dublin convincing himself he's worried about the nation when really it's only his guilt at selling out on the mushrooms and, at his lowest ebb, an encounter in the woods with Miz Moon. There he is again, later on the same night, crossing the school grounds, aching for the flesh pots. Just beyond the shadow of the new gym, aka the Ní Chuilleanáin Sports and Leisure Complex, he is stopped in his tracks by a lighted window and a nun sewing...

If you could die and come back as a poem, what poem would it be? Would I want to come back as one? All that work. The subterfuge, the creeping up unawares, the burrowing under skin. Given the hardship and unpleasantness involved, a poem has to be among the lower life forms, definitely more insect than god. And, no matter how beautiful or intricate or mysterious I was, would I really want to spend my days lugging around twice my body weight in accessories – knife sets, lotions, slow-release infusions? Assuming I did manage to put in enough sufficiently unwhole-some lifetimes to be reborn as a poem, and that I had the resolve to get back to human form asap, returning as James Merrill's 'Matinées' would probably be an efficient way of burning off the bad karma. Otherwise, for the quiet life, one where I'd be left alone to read my *Herald* in the corner of the café, it would have to be a Prynne.

Someone offers you €1,000,000 to never write again: What is your response? I would report the offer to the exiled contessa who came across my poems some years ago in one of the classier journals. Ever since, she's been sending me worshipping notes of encouragement along with a modest but far from measly monthly stipend. She would come up with a reason-able counter-offer, I'm sure. She knows what I'm trying to do.

It's the centenary of the Easter Rising: does this fact matter to you and if so, in what way? For better or worse, without the Rising I would be someone else. Elements of the darker side of nationalism were still very much in the air when I was growing up in the 1970s – enough to beget a childish fear, of unexpected sticking power, that I would never be able to make the grade as a bona fide Irishman. Music was a dreaming space against that, and, later, the Wexford Arts Centre, which was incredibly hospita-ble to a group of teenagers coming in off the street to put on plays and revues. In my twenties, seeing some of the Columban missionaries in action when I lived in Korea, and getting to know one in particular, gave me the education I then so badly needed in the meaning of freedom and standing up to overlords, outside and in.

You've arranged a date for 8pm, but it's 8.10pm now. You're working on a poem and it's going well. What do you do? The poetry wouldn't get a look-in. I'd be too busy primping, fretting about my hair.

Have you ever carried a poem by someone else around on your person? If so, what was it? Bernard Spencer's 'Boat Poem'. And, occasionally, when he has entrusted me with one, something new by my friend Pat Maddock.

A family member says, 'You should write a poem about that': what do you do? I slip out of my hermit's robes and do my little dance.

If your best poem were a weekend away, where would it be? The Bantry Chamber Music Festival.

Your friend is depressed: what's the very last poetry book you'd give him/her? Something afraid of its own shadow – anything with 'Reflections' in the title, or described on the back cover as poems that will put a smile on your face. I'd prefer to pass on my own volumes of Plath and Trakl, trusting that my friend would discover inside the shadows some of his/her banished brightness.

What's your current favourite word? Spatchcocked.

What advice would you give to older poets? I am older than a few 'older poets'. As reminders to myself, I would keep the words 'vim' and 'humourosity' close to my desk. Also a yoga mat, and a line by Charles Tomlinson warning of the 'soft oppression' of comfort. I would listen to lots of Janáček, especially the flood of masterpieces that came in his sixties and seventies.

You're given a choice: either every poem or no poem you write from now on must use the word 'I'. Which do you choose? Someone I know recently returned from a silent meditation retreat. She said that all that people seemed to be interested in was the silence – what was it like not being able to speak for a month? To her they had missed the point. The silence was just the means of getting to where she wanted to go – asking her about the silence was like asking a diver what it was like wearing a wet-suit. The speaker or person who is telling the poem – and often the subject matter as well – is a bit like the diving suit. If I feel 'my own' skin against the water, I'm probably in trouble.

Is there any question you wish you'd been asked here (that you'd like to answer now?) If I were asked what apart from the contessa sees me through, I'd say my three women.

Christodoulos Makris

TRYING TO COOK BREAKFAST...

trying to cook breakfast and type at same time
a classic 50s diner pile of pancakes kind of thing or a modern cup of
    coffee and a cigarette
with a clear blue sky ,Californian palm trees nearby, the blue ocean
    sparkling in the morning sun

just bacon , fried bread, egg, beans in a dingy English kitchen with a
    dull overcast day outside the window
makes me drift away on a lovely soft breeze

if I had a thousand mouths I'd kiss her all over, at the same time

Christodoulos Makris

IN '87 HUEY LEWIS...

In '87 Huey Lewis & The News released *Fore!*, their most accomplished album. I think their undisputed masterpiece is 'Hip To Be Square', a song so catchy most people probably don't listen to the lyrics. But they should, because it's not just about the pleasures of conformity, and the importance of trends, it's also a personal statement about the band itself.

Thank you, Patrick.

Their early work was a little too new wave for my tastes, but when *Sports* came out in '83 I think they really came into their own, commercially and artistically. The whole album has a clear, crisp sound, and a new sheen of consummate professionalism that really gives the songs a big boost. He's been compared to Elvis Costello, but I think Huey has a far more bitter, cynical sense of humour.

That's funny, because The News (minus Lewis) were the backing band on *My Aim Is True*.

As far as I recall, only one of the News played on *My Aim is True*.

Note: *All errors and inconsistencies in these poems are intentional.* – C.M.

Christodoulos Makris

Were you a strange child with a taste for verse? Early leanings towards artistic endeavour were overshadowed by my activities in sport, the impression that they're incompatible persisting until my twenties. Maybe I've grown into strangeness, a standing apart. The root of the word is key: one of my early formative texts, Albert Camus' *L'Étranger*, is widely translated as *The Outsider*.

Do you too dislike it? More often than I would like. Especially when it's steeped in a rigid understanding of what it is, what it can do or be. To borrow from curator Hans-Ulrich Obrist, a good definition of art, and in extension of poetry, could be 'that which expands the definition'.

If you could die and come back as a poem, what poem would it be? Frank O'Hara's 'Having a Coke with You' might be nice. A joyous investigation of love and art, and one of my sons' favourite poems. That way I shall stay close to them even after my premature demise.

Have you ever glued pages of a poetry book together? Making the 100 copies of my artist's book *Muses Walk* involved binding together printed cardboard sheets with string individually and by hand. My wife did a lot of that work though... I've also performed erasures on poetry books by others. Conversely, I was recently told that students at London's Kingston College cut my latest book up as an exercise in collaging. A friend wondered whether they'd manage to successfully turn it into a Victorian novel.

It's the centenary of the Easter Rising: does this fact matter to you and if so, in what way? A centenary is certainly a convenient mark to take stock. How the Rising is understood (and argued about) seems to revolve around a binary view of Ireland which I'm not sure is applicable anymore. And considering the range of crises the wider world is facing – social, moral, humanitarian and others – the overwhelming attention to it feels disproportionate and a little like burying our heads in the sand. In any case, I find readings of poetry through a national lens of little value. Several writers have commented on the 'kitsch-ness' of nationalism (and its more acceptable cousin, patriotism), the narrowness of perceiving writers according to national labels, and the feeling one sometimes gets during international festivals of taking part in Eurovision-style contests.

If someone described you as a political poet, what would your reaction be? I was in fact quite recently set to be described as a political poet in a brochure, something I rejected. Not that politics is absent from my work: on the contrary. But the 'political poet' brand carries echoes of polemic. A kind of writing steeped in certainty, its purpose to force its reader into assent. Whether I agree with the sentiment expressed or not, I tend to switch off pretty much immediately.

Would you rather be the poet or the poem? There's no choice: I am the poet. Question 3 notwithstanding.

If you could pick a time to be dropped amongst the three best poets alive at that moment, when would it be and who would they be? Hierarchies seem to me rather limiting, plus they deny access to pleasurable and empathy-enabling polyphonies. I feel our age parallels the post-first world war era to a considerable degree – so undermining ideologies as a loose element of European Dada might be both apt and fun. But I am in fact here and now, working in and responding to contemporary conditions. The rate of change that language and its use (tools, media, intention, et cetera). are currently undergoing is extraordinary. We're living in a particularly fertile time for poetry, and at a significant crossroads.

You've arranged a date for 8pm, but it's 8.10pm now. You're working on a poem and it's going well. What do you do? Send a message of apology to my date. Then put the poem away and get on the road. I like to respond to real life conditions and chance encounters, often inserting them into the writing, and though very serious about what I do I try to avoid getting precious about it.

A family member says, 'You should write a poem about that': what do you do? My younger son recently asked me to write a poem about Donald Trump. At the utterance of which my eldest advised me not to. The CIA, he said, would come after us.

If your best poem were a weekend away, where would it be? Next weekend.

It's a good poem but it's forty-one lines long and the competition with the big prize specifies a max of forty: what do you do? Nothing. I rarely enter those competitions. Sending work to magazines, journals, newspapers et cetera means entering into a form of competition, of course, but that's not determined by a conception of 'best'. Through my editorial work I understand that decisions are made on the basis of suitability to the outlet and issue-building considerations, among others. Besides, poems are not necessarily composed of lines. This isn't such a radical statement any more: one of the most decorated English language poetry books of last year, Claudia Rankine's *Citizen*, contains very few lines among its 160 or so pages.

You're given a choice: either every poem or no poem you write from now on must use the word 'I'. Which do you choose? I'm no longer interested in writing a version of autobiography in poetic form. We're a conflation of multiple, constantly evolving and often contradictory selves, and fixing a sense of the poet's personal identity into the poetry makes little sense. But I like constraint, and counter-intuition: so I'd take using it in every poem.

Who will play the poet in the Hollywood adaptation of your last poem? Christian Bale. Naturally.

You're proud of the poem but know it will offend someone you don't even like: what do you do? If I feel it works within the overall body of material it belongs to, and/or if individually it carries successfully, then I think nothing different to what I would do in the case of any other piece.

Would you rather win the TS Eliot Prize or the Prize Bonds? Winning a poetry prize is a nice form of recognition, though not a reliable measure of how necessary or influential the work is. And it's only an individual accolade. The Prize Bonds on the other hand would take care of much more than the poet.

Let's assume you're 60 and still publishing poems: what do you want to have achieved between now and then? I'd have already achieved it: I'd still be writing and publishing. Having even a small influence, whether through my compositional or editorial/curatorial work, on other poets or on how people perceive poetry, would be a frankly unexpected bonus.

What advice would you give to older poets? To look to those whose minds have remained inquisitive. None of us know how we'd react if our work and ideas become superseded by new concerns and new ways of working, but artists who remain relevant are never dismissive of the new. I write this with the news of David Bowie's death still fresh: a sparkling model for older artists, and young.

Geraldine Mitchell

WOMAN ALONE

When she wakes

darkness

five strokes
of a church bell
close-by   the room still
conceals its contours,
the narrow bed its thin quilt.

The brick floor grits underfoot
like blown sand
as she moves to the window,
pushes open shutters on air
smooth with the promise of heat.

The wake of the ringing
washes the walls of the cobbled street
and above furrowed rooftops
                stars
waver like sparks,
lustre the air with lost notes.

She leans on the sill, feels
the mystery of sound emerging
from silence, returning into it, of being
in time, then out of it,
        the thinning night,
how her day has been changed before it's begun
and no-one to know it but her.

Geraldine Mitchell

BURROW

All I see is the entrance
to the burrow of your
skull: two dark moons
defined by absence, desolate as
rock pools brimming
on the ebb tide of blind night.

Outside the world is loud, is bright, is
brash, is busy, is the crash of
cymbals. You curtain your eyes with
a fan of uncertain fingers.

The night has blown drifts
over the rest of your face,
sand fills your mouth and
marram grass catches
in the silt of grains.

The topography of dunes shifts
constantly. You wake to a new
geography, abandon the old map,
peer at the compass you have owned
for years, strange now, unfamiliar as a toy
rashly ordered on the internet.

The burrow holes are dark and
filled with absence. This morning
a full moon drifted down
the smooth October sky –
an ocular globe slipped of its orbit to
float to America, as fixed on its course
as the needle of the compass you hold.

From inside your dark hide
what did you see? What comfort
in that round, white, mottled
face?

Geraldine Mitchell

I decided I'd weave a seamless prose response to the questionnaire, a garment as dazzling as the *traje de luces* of my ideal poem. But bulbs blew, threads tangled and I sat night after night ripping what I had woven during the day.

The problem was putting it all into words. The irony of that. The deeper my involvement with poetry, the more private that world seems to become – not the content, not the resulting poem which is for 'out there', but my relationship with words themselves, the tracking and taming of them. Here it was about being anything but slant, it's the full frontal approach to those creatures we work with, that we coax, cajole, interrogate, choose, remove, recover, discard or subject to radical surgery.

So I've decided to answer the questions one by one after all, but to limit my answers to thirty words. Patchwork rather than seamless garment.

Were you a strange child with a taste for verse? Not strange, but the youngest and benignly neglected. Verse was 'Albert and the Lion', Dr Hoffmann's *Der Struwwelpeter* ... until polio closed primary school and an aunt temporarily home-schooled cousins and sisters.

Do you too dislike it? 'The Lady of Shallott', 'Kubla Khan', 'The Charge of the Light Brigade', the 'Ancient Mariner' at seven years old? What was there to dislike? It was performance poetry and fun.

Who is your favourite character in a poem? La Belle Dame Sans Merci had me in thrall very young, with her long hair and wild eyes. An encouraging reversal after the poor Shallott lady's fate. Such sounds, too.

If you could die and come back as a poem, what poem would it be? 'Donal Óg' (Lady Gregory's). I love the cadences and how it captures the human condition: yearning for a love as hopeless, pure and full of promise as the philosopher's stone.

Someone offers you €1,000,000 to never write again: What is your response? On the principle of no free lunches, I wouldn't take it anyway. But if I did, I could keep writing in my head and publish under a heteronym, like Pessoa.

It's the centenary of the Easter Rising: does this fact matter to you and if so, in what way? A lot. For the tragic loss of brutally executed leaders; for betrayed ideals. Arbour Hill with Michael Biggs's carving of the Proclamation is a good place to meditate on this.

If someone described you as a political poet, what would your reaction be? I read and write poetry; I am alive and, hopefully, alert. CK Williams called poetry the 'moral resonance of the world'. If I can be part of that, I'm happy.

Would you rather be the poet or the poem? Being the poem I will be the poet, too, if Michael Donaghy's 'alchemical payoff' has taken place – those rare occasions when the poem seems to have written itself. Pure gold.

If you could pick a time to be dropped amongst the three best poets alive at that moment, when would it be? If I could have the poets without the cruel moment, it would be Lorca, Machado and Hernández. Otherwise the US mid-twentieth century with Elizabeth Bishop, Ruth Stone and Amy Clampitt.

Have you ever carried a poem by someone else around on your person? Mahon's 'The Mayo Tao' at one point, but the one I've carried longest is Samuel Menashe's 'Cargo': 'Old wounds leave good hollows'… A poem as watertight as a ship's hold.

If your best poem were a weekend away, where would it be? A rambling stone farmhouse in the Pyrenees. Logs, rugs, wine, wind and snow. Alone? Maybe, maybe not. Sheep and goats' bells from across the steep valley. Deep sleep. Fleet dreams.

It's a good poem but it's forty-one lines long and the competition with the big prize specifies a max of forty: what do you do? Have another look at the poem. There are probably line breaks that could be improved. Or hope the judges will be so blown away that they won't stop to count.

Have you ever used a poem to seduce someone? If so, what poem was it? (And did it work?) Never to seduce, though I have been on the receiving end. I wrote a poem in anger and revenge one time and it only made matters a whole lot worse.

You're given a choice: either every poem or no poem you write from now on must use the word 'I'. Which do you choose? I'd definitely go with the 'I', which I see as a hitching post or Shaker peg to hang the poem's heart on. It needn't have anything to do with autobiography.

Your friend is depressed: what's the very last poetry book you'd give him/her? Edited by Carolyn Forché, *Against Forgetting: Twentieth Century Poetry of Witness.* This magnificent anthology of the poetry of oppression and war is devastating testimony to man's relentless inhumanity to man.

What's your current favourite word? Lattermath, a rural English dialect word for aftermath used by Edward Thomas in 'It Was Upon…' It chimes with a word my husband took to using – *elseplace* – for somewhere else.

You're proud of the poem but know it will offend someone you don't even like: what do you do? I tend not to write poems about real live people, but I think in general I agree with Elizabeth Bishop's reproach to Robert Lowell: Art just isn't worth that much.

Let's assume you're 60 and still publishing poems: what do you want to have achieved between now and then? That assumption is past fulfilment for me. But I've no intention of stopping getting published. The aim always is to write better poems – and the goalposts are eternally receding.

Cyril Connolly said the true function of a writer is to write a masterpiece and no other task is of any consequence. Do you agree? How masculine is *masterpiece*! The poet's function is to love words, be open to learning and to listen – to herself, to the world, to the shriek of melting icebergs.

If your ideal poem were an outfit, what would it look like? A *traje de luces*, the bullfighter's costume, with lights and colours and a dimmer switch. Colours ranging from the scarlet of a sheep's placenta to tawny bog grass in November.

What advice would you give older poets? What do I say to myself every morning? Stop watching for your reflection in other poets' work. Learn to trust your own. The poets who shout loudest aren't always right.

Is there any question you wish you'd been asked here (that you'd like to answer now?) 'O thin men of Haddam, / Why do you imagine golden birds? / Do you not see how the blackbird / Walks around the feet / Of the women about you?' – Wallace Stevens.

Julie Morrissy

REMOVAL

the city has been giving me the silent treatment
for one hundred and eighty-two days
because I refuse to give it the attention it deserves

one hundred and eighty-two days of protection
from the harshness of its words in a language
I certainly speak but cannot understand

the wind carries words so fast
whipping meanings away from me
when all I am doing is trying

to park my rental car overnight
make sense of the instructions on the sign
the horror on the minus thirty-five morning

when the car is gone – vanished
dumped two blocks away
in Little Portugal

you hand me a ticket;
by the end of April you soften
know you have been cruel, realise that maybe

you and I can make it
because the swings in Parc Jeanne-Mance
have been hung up again

and the Bixis are slotted back into position;
I still test each step of the spiral walk-up
holding onto the railing for dear life

Julie Morrissy

THE FAMINE ROAD
    – for Eavan Boland

there are shells of bodies on the other side too
in Ireland Park
I've heard stories of Harry and Paul
wandering around that island
escaping from a downtown Toronto hotel
to see personalities set in stone
on both sides of the Atlantic

we don't need a statue now
the Irish buzz around the T Dot like natives
I see them at brunch in Roncy
at the boutiques on Queen
mixology lessons at the Drake Hotel
their personalities, a different kind of stone

a brighter one
our passports, a bargaining chip
c'mere and we do a swap
we give our educations, the letters after our names
they give healthcare, vitality, youth
– promise

weekends to the cottage
late breaks to New York City
I ask Joan if she wants to go
for a quick run to Brooklyn
a summer jaunt

do you think they let Kenyans in
without a visa?

Do you?

Julie Morrissy

It's the centenary of the Easter Rising: does this fact matter to you and if so, in what way? Yes, the Rising matters to me. I persist in questioning the power structures that surround us, not just in this country but globally. I believe it is important to stand up for your beliefs and not only to voice them but also to act. It is very difficult to take on the power of government but I believe there is strength in the grassroots. My work as an activist for the Repeal of the 8th Amendment and human rights for women in Ireland is inspired by people who have similarly acted for change in the past.

If someone described you as a political poet, what would your reaction be? My current project, a hybrid book-length poem, engages significantly with postmodern poetics and is notably influenced by the work of CD Wright, Claudia Rankine, and M. NourbeSe Philip. As theorists like Linda Hutcheon note, the postmodern aesthetic is inescapably political and inherently historical and social. I see the poem in the same way as Lyn Hejinian does; a field for inquiry that has the ability to improve the world. That improvement is a process. I am interested in poetry that reaches outward and has the power to influence how readers orient themselves to the world. Language is biased and political by its very nature. The way we speak about things, whether in poetry or elsewhere, reveals the power dynamics in operation in daily life. In my view, it is difficult to speak at all without being 'political'.

Would you rather be the poet or the poem? I think being the poem is more liberating. The poem can do what it has to do and I think it can get away with more than the person sometimes.

If you could pick a time to be dropped amongst the three best poets alive at that moment, when would it be and who would they be? I thought I was in the best time until CD Wright's recent passing. My most important influences are living writers whom I have either had the privilege of knowing or who I have studied intensely. I am really interested in the Language Poets, the New York School and the Black Mountain poets, many of whom are still alive. I suppose I would choose to be dropped in the late 1960s Language movement with Lyn Hejinian, Susan Howe, Barrett Watten and those guys.

You've arranged a date for 8pm, but it's 8.10pm now. You're working on a poem and it's going well. What do you do? Get up and go. Sometimes it is beneficial to step away even when the writing is going well. And living my life is at least as important and as fun as writing about it.

A family member says, 'You should write a poem about that': what do you do?
People say this kind of thing to writers and artists frequently. I get a lot
of it especially because my poems tend to feature things like McDonald's
menu items, kitchen utensils, dead animals and such. So far, I haven't
written a poem on someone else's suggestion…

*It's a good poem but it's forty-one lines long and the competition with the big
prize specifies a max of forty: what do you do?* Probably move two lines
together and send it. Sometimes it pays to be practical.

*You're given a choice: either every poem or no poem you write from now on must
use the word 'I'. Which do you choose?* I would get rid of the 'I', not because
my poems don't often rely on subjectivity but because it would be more
of a challenge and it would develop my poetry in a different way. Let's
hope it never comes to this though.

Have you ever glued pages of a poetry book together? No. Underlining things is
the extent of my defacement.

Someone offers you €1,000,000 to never write again: What is your response?
How closely will I be monitored?

Who will play the poet in the Hollywood adaptation of your last poem? Cush
Jumbo.

*You're invited to read in a major festival: what are your top three backstage
demands?* Do poets get to make backstage demands? Kraken and Coke.
Ham. The icing part of the cake. I guess I know now for next time.

*You're proud of the poem but know it will offend someone you don't even like:
what do you do?* This happens sometimes. I would publish it but not
preform it at readings. Depending on how upset the person is, that might
influence where I publish the poem. It is not always obvious what or
whom my poems are about so I would tell them to take solace in the fact
that nobody will ever think it is about them.

Would you rather win the TS Eliot Prize or the Prize Bonds? TS Eliot. Any
excuse to wear velvet for an occasion.

*Let's assume you're 60 and still publishing poems: what do you want to have
achieved between now and then?* I want to have read a lot more, and of
course, I want to write more manuscripts/collections. I would also love
to build my poetry community transatlantically. Because I have spent

much of the last decade living in North America, my relationships with Canadian and American poets have come to mean a lot to me personally and to my practice. I hope that in the next thirty years (!) I can strengthen those ties with the view to expanding perspectives on poetry both in North America and in Ireland. I wouldn't mind being part of a 'school' either but you have to think of a really good name.

Cyril Connolly said the true function of a writer is to write a masterpiece, and no other task is of any consequence. Do you agree? For me, it is more about progress and development. I want to make sure I'm pushing myself into new spaces, themes and ways of working. Writing, for me, is about constantly improving and re-improving.

If your ideal poem were an outfit, what would it look like? A nurse's outfit.

What advice would you give to older poets? I can't really imagine giving advice to older poets. Probably just to get a good website.

Emma Must

SNEDDING

Mornings in the dusty wood
we'd take a hand-axe, hack
a mouth into the trunk a foot
or so above the base, take care to gauge
where it would fall, then with this word,
as new and sharp to me as *billhook*,
clear the lower branches – sliced clean off
if you pitch the angle well,
come at it with a deft wrist flick,
but snagging now and then on knots
or rather on the complex places limb
and timber join, becoming only later
those dark eyes that give the tree –
now cut and dried and stacked
in planks – its second beauty.

Emma Must

ROOM AIR

He likes jazz, I tell the nurse, and blues, so the radio plays low inside
    the heavy-curtained cubicle.
The concentration of oxygen delivered through his ventilator will be
    reduced to 21 per cent,
then he'll be breathing what we breathe. This will end his life. She
    angles his monitor
so I cannot watch the numbers drop. We begin. I have no idea for
    how long.

A song comes on from where I now call home: *Hey where did we go,*
    days when the rains came? ...
From beyond the muddy estuaries and sea loughs, that reclaimed
    land – its flats and silts –
this rush of other air ushers in a sweep of glens, those little islands I
    have never visited,
and what is left when lengths of peat are stripped from bogs across
    the uplands –

lesions paling on the hill's dark chest – the smudge of shadow pointing
    west behind each rowan
in each windbreak, a quarry swallowing the space of seven fields,
    then, as if you were flying
somewhere, say, and coming in to land, the way the quarry folds
    into itself behind its lip...
Thank you for everything, I tell him again. *Do you remember when we*
    used to sing?

Sha la la la la la la la la la la te da ... that yellow submarine moored on
    the Lagan, the very river,
its upper reaches curving through marshes, under the Red Bridge,
    then divvied up by locks
and sluices, its exuberance curtailed by brick, and back and back
    until we've come full
circle to the Giant's Ring: a prehistoric cicatrix, a valve, a stopping
    place, a lung.

Emma Must

Were you a strange child with a taste for verse? Yes. I fell in love with Heaney at school, then Larkin. At Brownies, aged seven, I got into a tussle with the Writer Badge assessor over my use of the word 'teasel' in a poem. She said it wasn't a word; I begged to differ. Aged ten, I was Highly Commended in a *Daily Mirror* competition for a poem about electricity pylons, imaginatively titled 'Metal Giants'...

Do you too dislike it? No, I love it. It is the most important thing in my life. As for poets, I do try to dilute them a bit with more linear-brained people such as engineers, astrophysicists, landscape gardeners, etc. In a nice way.

Someone offers you €1,000,000 to never write again: What is your response? Keep your money.

Have you ever glued pages of a poetry book together? No. Why would you want to do that?

It's the centenary of the Easter Rising: does this fact matter to you and if so, in what way? I'm always interested in acts of rebellion against forces of oppression. Sometimes you just have to take a stand. I've been reading up on the history of the Easter Rising, and I'll be following the coverage of the centenary events.

If someone described you as a political poet, what would your reaction be? This subject interests me a lot. I wouldn't object to being described that way, but I might go on to explore the idea a bit further... I was a full-time activist on environment and development issues for about ten years until 2002 when I took the active decision to stop being an activist and to focus on writing poetry. The two activities occupied the same part of my brain and I couldn't do both at once. Despite – for me – the locus of creativity being identical, politics and poetry are not at all the same thing. Politics is social, and it requires quick decisions and actions for as long as it takes to achieve your ends. Poetry requires time, layering and reflection; it is most authentic when done without any specific purpose in mind (otherwise it usually becomes polemic); and it is a solitary activity (albeit benefiting absolutely from being surrounded by an active poetry culture, such as exists in Belfast right now, for example). That's not to say that poetry can't deal with political issues, or be subsequently used in the service of political ends. It certainly can. If you want to generate specific political change, you'd be better off devising a strategy, writing a press release, organising an action, and... and... and... You won't have time to sit and write poetry. Nevertheless, to quote Auden elegising Yeats: poetry 'survives', it is 'a way of happening, a mouth'.

What's your worst poetry habit? Over-using colons. I'm trying to wean myself off them, but it's the way my brain works: it makes me happy, to quote Fowler: 'delivering the goods that have been invoiced in the preceding words'.

You've arranged a date for 8pm, but it's 8.10pm now. You're working on a poem and it's going well. What do you do? I don't date. It's a waste of valuable writing time.

Have you ever carried a poem by someone else around on your person? If so, what was it? Yes, last week. 'Canopy' by Emily Berry. I heard it on *The Echo Chamber* on Radio 4, tracked it down online and printed it off. '[A]nd they said they would' is such a great ending for a poem about wanting to be looked after by trees.

Have you ever used a poem to seduce someone? If so, what poem was it? (And did it work?) Oh God. No. But I know poets who have.

You're given a choice: either every poem or no poem you write from now on must use the word 'I'. Which do you choose? Every.

You're invited to read in a major festival: what are your top three backstage demands? I try really hard not to be demanding. It's a trait I don't much like in myself, so I try to minimise it – with varying degrees of success. A bottle of water, maybe?

What's your current favourite word? Grattoir (noun. a scraper made of flint).

You're proud of the poem but know it will offend someone you don't even like: what do you do? Publish and be damned. It's a much more difficult decision if you like the person.

Let's assume you're 60 and still publishing poems: what do you want to have achieved between now and then? I turn 50 this year and – as is quite often the case for female poets – am only now getting properly into my stride, so I sincerely hope I'll still be publishing poems in ten years' time. (Three cheers to *Poetry Ireland Review* for not defining 'generation' in terms of age, by the way). I'm so excited that poetry is finally at the centre of my life. I just want to keep on steadily writing collections. I've got the first one mapped out and two-thirds written, the next one partially planned, and a clear idea for the one after that… Here's to writing!

'The hard part is getting to the top of page 1' – Tom Stoppard. *What, for you, is the hard part?* Growing up. Though I am definitely getting there.

If your ideal poem were an outfit, what would it look like? A tailored Sixties dress. With red lipstick.

What advice would you give to older poets? Fewer humorous ditties about your contemporaries. Fewer bums, tits and fannies.

Is there any question you wish you'd been asked here (that you'd like to answer now?) Is it a problem that female poets are often under-represented in many arenas, including magazines and journals, and schemes to promote new writers? Yes, it is. Editors and organisers: aim for 50:50, and actively seek more submissions from female poets, if necessary. If *Poetry* Magazine in Chicago can do this, then we can do this in Ireland too.

Doireann Ní Ghríofa

LINES WRITTEN ON SPINAL MORPHINE

Call it a hospital and it is,
but call it a hive and it splits
into divisions where we become bees,
hovering, nectar-flecked, through
a multi-storied maze where we flit and fizz.

Plump honeybees, we flicker through
dawn-dark corridors to the distant rooms
of Neonatal ICU. We limp, all bristling
stitches, morphine drips, engorgements,
shuffling to incubators clotted with knots of new.

There, our breath is gas on glass
where small hands grasp
at air. We wince when we sit by our infants,
grimace over our bruised inner throbs, our queried clots,
our weeping insides, our leaking gasps.

At night, the hive pulses with the buzz
of breast-pumps, dull drone of rush and suck
and we stumble-glide through corridors
on bruised wings, gripping phials of yellow nectar.
Below, in soft brood chambers, our young wait for us.

We are a swarm of bees, of which I am only one
and you are another, my final child, girl of honey-spun tulle.
I fill your ears with new words, let my voice become
the first to touch your spiralled cochlea.
I say: *froth* and *cusp*, say: *rushed* and *blood*,

I tremble and say: *cloud* and *dandelion* and *plum*.
All night I goo and gaw in your sleeping ear, clumps
of words spilling from me, a mess of morphine-jumbled
syllables. And oh my love, imagine all the floors above us
that brim and buzz. Can you hear the chorus we have become?

Doireann Ní Ghríofa

DRANNADH

Chuimhnigh mé ort, sínte siar i do leaba ospidéil
nuair a chonaic mé strainséir san fhoraois inné,

cú lena chois aige, srianta ar choniall leathair.
Nuair a chuala sé corraí sna neantóga,

scaoil sé dá iall é. Phreab a mhadra ar chlé, imithe
de ráib tríd an choill. Shíl mé go raibh sé ar strae

go dtí go bhfaca mé é, agus ina bhéal, coileáinín sionnaigh
scréachach a chaointe   ciúnaithe

ag drannadh an mhadra, fuaim a mhatáin á sracadh,
a chnámha beaga briste amhail cipíní scriosta,

agus pus an ghadhair fliuch-dearg. Bhreathnaigh mé
ar an bhfear i ngan fhios dó – níor fhág

an straois a bhéal agus é ag féachaint ar an mbás beag roimhe.
Lig sé fead ghlaice ar a mhadra gur fhill sé lena shála,

cuma mhúinte shibhialta arís air. Chuimhnigh mé
ar an ngalar a réab do chorp, greim na fiacaile aige ort,

agus mise i mo shuí taobh leat san ospidéal, ag breathnú
ar an ár a imríodh ort, do chorp craptha faoina ualach.

Stán mé, ní ort i do dhaonnacht, ach ar ghluaiseacht an ghalair,
an foréigean a tharraing gruaig ó do cheann agus cumhacht ó do
    mhatáin

agus mise, an cladhaire a shuigh ann gan teacht i gcabhair ort, mise
a bhreathnaigh ar do bhás,   i mo thost.

Doireann Ní Ghríofa

Were you a strange child with a taste for verse? I was definitely strange, but my taste for verse only hit me in my teenage years when I was given a brilliant anthology, *Real Cool* edited by Niall MacMonagle. The cover featured the sort of tall, battered Doc boots that I coveted in those grungy days of the mid-nineties. This book split me open to the wonders of poetry, with poems like Sharon Olds's 'The Moment', Denise Levertov's 'Leaving Forever' and Adrienne Rich's 'Aunt Jennifer's Tigers'. One poem that absolutely blew my teenage mind was 'The Pattern' by Paula Meehan, a poem that I'm still in awe of. I always say that parents should beware giving this book to teenagers unless they want a writer in the family – it's a gateway drug.

Do you too dislike it? No, Marianne, I adore it.

Someone offers you €1,000,000 to never write again: What is your response? I'd take the money and pay someone to transcribe spoken verse from me – there's always a way to break a rule. You could do too much good with that amount of money to ever consider turning it down.

Have you ever glued pages of a poetry book together? No. Some of the poems I have disliked at a first reading have grown on me in time. It'd be like gluing pages of an atlas together – the hidden page would become more interesting for having been forbidden.

It's the centenary of the Easter Rising: does this fact matter to you and if so, in what way? It does, deeply, in an oblique way. I've been thinking a lot about language, and how saddened those who participated in the Rising would be at the treatment of Irish today. That has led me to considering, and writing around, our linguistic history.

If someone described you as a political poet, what would your reaction be? I'd be very pleased that they had read my work so attentively.

Would you rather be the poet or the poem? The creator or the creation? The former, I'd rather create than be the static creation. I'd rather be the *cailleach* than the enchantment.

What's your worst poetry habit? A terrible compulsion to keep changing poems after they've been published. I tinker and tinker, it's incessant.

You've arranged a date for 8 pm, but it's 8.10pm now. You're working on a poem and it's going well. What do you do? I've never been on a date!

Have you ever carried a poem by someone else around on your person? If so, what was it? Yes. I carry 'Train Ride' by Ruth Stone around with me, like a talisman.

If your best poem were a weekend away, where would it be? A very old lane-way in an inner city, dilapidated and filthy.

It's a good poem but it's forty-one lines long and the competition with the big prize specifies a max of forty: what do you do? Take out the last two lines. I tend to write an extra two lines of a sort of bizarre summary on some poems, it's redundant.

Have you ever used a poem to seduce someone? If so, what poem was it? (And did it work?) Hah! No. My other half hates poetry so reading him a poem would be the opposite of a seduction!

You're given a choice: either every poem or no poem you write from now on must use the word 'I'. Which do you choose? I'd take 'I'. You could always disguise it as Roman numerals in the title.

Who will play the poet in the Hollywood adaptation of your last poem? Maggie Gyllenhaal, as her character in Lenny Abrahamson's *Frank*. She's a strange combination of mad and cranky, just like many of my poems (and me).

You're invited to read in a major festival: what are your top three backstage demands? Coffee, coffee, coffee…

What's your current favourite word? Ossicle / flichreoch.

You're proud of the poem but know it will offend someone you don't even like: what do you do? Be true to the work.

Would you rather win the TS Eliot Prize or the Prize Bonds? Easy, prize bonds – the type of work I write would never be chosen for an English prize. I'd spend some of the money on publishing poetry pamphlets for new writers in Ireland. There are so many exciting new voices emerging (I won't name names, you know who you are!) and it's an important part of a writer's development to have a concrete publication of your work. It helps you grow.

Let's assume you're 60 and still publishing poems: what do you want to have achieved between now and then? An interesting body of work. I've always been driven by the presence of death, and felt it breathing on my neck. It's part of what drives me as a writer – if I died tomorrow, would I have left a body of work I could be proud of? (The answer is always no, that's what keeps you running. New poems lose their lustre so fast, so you just keep chasing the high, one of many ways in which poetry is like a Class A habit). I deeply admire the Aisteach Project, coordinated by Dr Jennifer Walshe as a thought experiment to create an (imaginary) archive of the Irish avant garde. Reading it, I was struck by the sense of a body of work that can be created in a lifetime. I hope that the body of work I will have produced by the end of my life will be as interesting and as strange as some of those in the Aisteach Project (**www.aisteach.org**).

Cyril Connolly said the true function of a writer is to write a masterpiece, and no other task is of any consequence. Do you agree? I think a writer has to be true to her art, and try to write her own masterpiece within her own parameters, to please only herself. No one should be writing for a 'canon' or trying to conform to the expectations of others. Be true to your own self, that's where your best work lives.

'The hard part is getting to the top of page 1' – Tom Stoppard. What, for you, is the hard part? Childcare. With four children under seven, procrastination is a luxury I cannot indulge.

If your ideal poem were an outfit, what would it look like? Spiky.

What advice would you give to older poets? Take the time to encourage a younger writer. We're all in this mess together.

Mary Noonan

BODY

We never touched, all the years
of our long story, kept our distance.
Your cheekbone – chiselled, bristly –
was a strange land. Even the word body
was banned – it never left your mouth.
But now I'm all over you, an octopus
popping pills on your tongue at breakfast,
allowing your false teeth to plop
into my palm at night. I lather soap
on your salt-and-pepper skin, draw
the blade slowly over your jaw, waver
round the small apple. I undress you,
open the shower door, prod you in.
I beg you to send your hand back out,
squeeze shampoo on your palm,
urge you to rub it into your scalp.
You shiver, cringe, tell me my hands
are icy cold. I never thought I'd see
my father's penis. And after the long haul
of hours spent cajoling you to lie down
under the covers, you grab my hand,
lock it in yours, won't let it go.

Mary Noonan

OCTOBER JAZZ

The crows are lining up on the scalloped roof
of the old church – a long row of monks
gossiping, squabbling. It's the hour when the dog
goes home, and the wolf comes out, the hour the clocks
shuttled backward last night.

Almost Samhain, the time of burials and unearthings,
and the city is teeming with jazz musicians.
But here, on this hill, I'm like a sole survivor,
swimming slowly through the thick silence
that hangs in the air after the dust has settled.

As I pass the church, I turn and see myself,
in the silence, twenty years earlier,
in my new duck-egg-blue silk shirt and
my black high-heeled suede boots, all set
to storm the jazzy town, hopped-up

on the adrenalin of a day spent spritzing
the house, putting fresh sheets on the bed,
fresh-cut flowers in the bowl, ready for
the man I'll meet at the concert, prepared
to be surprised by the dancer who will find me

among the sweating bodies squeezing to the bar.
I'm the bystander, the one wanting to run
from the crepe soles squelching in beer-soaked pile.
And I do. Out of the silence I come, clambering back
up the hill, past the church, past midnight.

No crows, but a radiant moon, a midnight-blue sky,
stars playing ten pin bowling and riffing on Mingus's
'Wednesday Night Prayer Meeting', brass hounds
growling round my brain. The first frost is stinging
my earlobes, hairs are standing up along my legs.

Clambering back, the decades-lighter-me
vaporises into the twilight, and I give the friary of crows
a last look, walk on.

Mary Noonan

Were you a strange child with a taste for verse? I was probably strange, not sure about the taste for verse. I did like words, and remember the thrill of realising I could read the notices on the bus! I had a big book called *A Treasury of Stories and Verse* when I was about seven. I remember reading about someone being 'on the horns of a dilemma' and asking what that meant.

If you could die and come back as a poem, what poem would it be? 'The Moose', by Elizabeth Bishop.

Someone offers you €1,000,000 to never write again: What is your response? I'd accept the money, willingly. Who'd be a poet? Are the poets you know generally happy people? No. Get out while the going is good. I'd take the money and move to a beautiful house somewhere warm, probably the South of France. I'd consider buying a vineyard and learning how to make wine. Now there's an occupation! My pinot noir would become legendary, and I'd sit in the sun drinking it and reading from my huge poetry library. Poetry needs more readers. And after all, when done right, reading is akin to writing.

It's the centenary of the Easter Rising: does this fact matter to you and if so, in what way? I was taken to Kilmainham Gaol on a school tour as a child in primary school. They pointed to the bullet-holes in the walls, and I remember being impressed. I was a romantic child, and the potent mix of nationalism and Catholicism really got to me – I believed in it all, fervently. Some part of me still admires what the small group of rebels did in 1916 – it was such a lost cause. Poets, intellectuals, teachers, risking all for an ideal. Well, we got our republic, but the violence meted out to the people – and their language and culture – in the pre-Republic past did not go away, it simply went underground, to re-emerge in manifold forms of power abuse within the Republic. The centenary has shown me that it takes a long, long time for extensive brutality to be redressed. Perhaps by 2116 Ireland's story will have evolved.

If someone described you as a political poet, what would your reaction be? I'd be surprised. I don't want a poem to have designs on me as a reader, or to have an obvious message, to be too obviously in the service of a cause or an agenda. Of course there are good political poems, but they're rare, and extremely difficult to write (I think of Yeats, Carolyn Forché). The personal is political. If we categorise poems into political and non-political, the labelling does something to everyone concerned, writer and reader. To label is to appropriate to oneself, to make assimilable, accessible. The labelled poem sits in the box of political poems, its meanings limited and constrained. It is no longer free to range just beyond our reach.

Would you rather be the poet or the poem? The poem. Poems have more fun. If luck is on the poem's side, and it has a good mother or father, it can go to the edges of being in ways that conscious-mind-driven humans cannot. Like dreams, a poem can hop about in time and space, change gender and age, perform egregious acts of violence on its rivals. Like small children, a poem can act as if the world is there to be eaten. When a poem smiles, its entire face cracks in two, and when a poem is sad or un-happy, the whole world knows about it. A poem can break all the rules, and still be loved. And if its mother or father are exceptional (but this is rare), a poem can live forever, or at least five hundred years.

If you could pick a time to be dropped amongst the three best poets alive at that moment, when would it be and who would they be? I'd like to be spirited into Robert Lowell's poetry seminar at Boston University in 1959, plonked between Sylvia Plath and her rival Anne Sexton, and then after the seminar, to go with the two women to the Ritz Carlton hotel to discuss Lowell's ideas and get drunk on martinis.

Have you ever carried a poem by someone else around on your person? If so, what was it? 'Soap Suds' by Louis MacNeice.

A family member says, 'You should write a poem about that': what do you do? Ignore them.

If your best poem were a weekend away, where would it be? Arizona, featuring the desert and a mule-ride along the terraces of the Grand Canyon: stark, unforgiving, and very high drama.

What's your current favourite word? Scuttle.

You're proud of the poem but know it will offend someone you don't even like: what do you do? I would be uncomfortable with the thought that some-one would feel personally targeted, in a malicious or vindictive way, by a poem I had written, and I would probably try not to publish it. But then I read Plath's 'Leaving Early' and I think: I'd sell my granny to write a poem like that!

Cyril Connolly said the true function of a writer is to write a masterpiece, and no other task is of any consequence. Do you agree? Yes, but few writers deliver the masterpiece. Which is what I remind myself whenever I'm in a hurry with my writing, or trying to get it published: how many poems of Keats or Coleridge does the world really remember? It only takes one poem, really, to make you a household name forever! So quality, not quantity. There are many writing tasks to be undertaken on the road to Shangri-La. And learning the craft is not nothing.

If your ideal poem were an outfit, what would it look like? The outfit worn by the Red Queen in Lewis Carroll's *Through the Looking-Glass*. Queen of the chess board, she wore blue queen eye shadow, a red-and-black dress with large white collar, tan corset, red dress-skirt with gold-black hearts, black shoes with red hearts under the heels, white-and-black striped stockings with red hearts, pearl necklace, and a gold crown with rubies.

What advice would you give to older poets? What's all this about older and younger poets? Does age matter in poetry? But if you mean poets who've been on the road a long time, I'd say keep going, and try to keep re-inventing yourself. Be wary of becoming a caricature of yourself: look at what the younger poets are doing, take sustenance from some of that. Listen to your heart and body and realise that at 70, you can't write the poems you wrote when you were 20. The magical thing about poetry is that it can give voice to a body and mind, whatever its age. And poetry doesn't make value judgements between the poems of youth and the poems of age.

Rebecca O'Connor

BIRD BELLING

There's a bird belling in the eaves of the house.
We look up at the ceiling because for some reason
it sounds like it's in the centre of the room –
     like a huge tweeting light bulb –
and we're surprised not to see it.

At the same time I'm wondering how many people
will find themselves writing about the woman
who accidentally joined a search party for herself.

And should I give a kidney to Hugo Williams?
I can't remember if I'm blood type O...
     And there is a risk.

I can't take risks with two small children.

The boys saw the dog kill a baby rabbit
out in the woods this afternoon.

I tried to encourage B to show some emotion –
Didn't it make you sad seeing that poor tiny fluffy little thing...?

     But no. He's a bit like Matisse in his final years
with his bright strips of paper and his scissors.

I am his Lydia, sweeping up after him,
preparing his crackers and cheese.

His little brother calls out, 'Mummy, Mummy, I'm crying!'
to which I reply, 'I have no idea where I am.'

Rebecca O'Connor

You hold the plectrum like a wren.
I am in love with your teacher, his fingers.

Once I found an egg in my jumper on the bedroom floor
after returning from a weekend in Oxford.

I picture it blue. That is how delicate this is –

not like the two pigs electrocuted in a pool of water under a tree,
one of them killed instantly, the other slowly grilled.

How like love this is – the girl in the next room singing
When the dog bites, when the bee stings, the *ting ting ting* on the piano.

My favourite thing is you. No,
not just you – your brother too!

And I love that our address is Above the Hairdressers, Main Street,
      Cootehill.
No postcode. It means, of course, I can buy nothing online

but I can live frugally. There's a fruit and vegetable shop next door
that sells a dozen duck eggs for under four euro.

Free haircuts sometimes too.

I grow my hair long. It grows quickly,
at pace with the metronome's *tick tock tick tock* –
        the wren plucking at the strings to make birdsong
– for it's broken, I cannot stop it.

Rebecca O'Connor

Were you a strange child with a taste for verse? I don't know if I was strange, but I was extremely shy. I loved music. I can remember singing myself to sleep at night (the theme song to Grizzly Adams, that kind of thing). And I loved dancing. *Top of the Pops* was a highlight of the week. I cried when Johnny Logan won the Eurovision with 'What's Another Year'. The first book I read (after Read-it-Yourselfs) was probably a children's bible I got for my first holy communion. And then a gift of *A Treasury of Verse* by Enid Blyton sparked off my first poem at the age of about eight. It was about a fairy.

Do you too dislike it? Poetry? Most of what I read, yes. But I wouldn't be trying to write it if I didn't love the form. The bad poems make you think you could do better and the good ones make you think you shouldn't even try. Stuck between a rock and a hard place.

Who is your favourite character in a poem? The poet.

If you could die and come back as a poem, what poem would it be? 'Do not go gentle into that good night'. Raging against death after dying and coming back as a poem about death would be a laugh. As long as the poem could then die and come back again as me.

Someone offers you €1,000,000 to never write again: What is your response? I'd have to think about it. Could I write songs? If I could write songs, then yes, I'll take the money. Otherwise no. Though if I was forced to take the money then I would probably have a go at painting. And who would ever know I was composing poems in my head? Would the thought police be involved in this scenario?

Have you ever glued pages of a poetry book together? Not that I recall.

It's the centenary of the Easter Rising: does this fact matter to you and if so, in what way? A few members of the IRB take it upon themselves to organise an insurrection at a time when Britain is sending tens of thousands to fight in the First World War. Most of those killed during the Rising are civilians. And, glory be, out of the embers rises Sinn Féin! I find it offensive that millions is being spent so that the country can literally make a song and dance of this.

If someone described you as a political poet, what would your reaction be? I'd say they were thinking of a different Rebecca O'Connor. And not the one who sings Tina Turner covers or writes about parrots either.

Would you rather be the poet or the poem? Definitely the poet.

If you could pick a time to be dropped amongst the three best poets alive at that moment, when would it be and who would they be? 1950s. Sylvia Plath, Elizabeth Bishop, Robert Lowell. I think... I suppose if I were stalking them, Boston would be a good place to start. Sitting in on Lowell's seminars, trying to make friends with Sylvia.

What's your worst poetry habit? Not writing.

You've arranged a date for 8pm, but it's 8.10pm now. You're working on a poem and it's going well. What do you do? I print off a copy of the draft and jot down notes. If it's going well then it will carry on going well in my head. And I apologise for being late, of course. Blame the children.

Have you ever carried a poem by someone else around on your person? If so, what was it? Yes, but I'm not saying.

If your best poem were a weekend away, where would it be? On a campsite in Connemara with my husband and three children, with a view of the tidal island of Omey. In the evenings we'd eat sausages (bought from the butcher's in Claddaghduff) and cooked on an open fire, and we'd drink lukewarm cans of Guinness as we watched the light sink into the Atlantic.

It's a good poem but it's forty-one lines long and the competition with the big prize specifies a max of forty: what do you do? That would be bad luck, as my poems are generally very short. I'd try to shrink it into 40 lines, but I probably wouldn't like it and have to put it back the way it was. Then I'd kick myself. Then I'd tell myself I'll enter next year. I might have another poem written by then.

Have you ever used a poem to seduce someone? If so, what poem was it? (And did it work?) I quoted poetry in letters I wrote to a boy when I was 15. Keats, probably. And some lines from poems in an old anthology of *Love Poems of the Irish* that was lying around the house. I think it frightened him off, ultimately.

You're given a choice: either every poem or no poem you write from now on must use the word 'I'. Which do you choose? I, I, I.

Your friend is depressed: what's the very last poetry book you'd give him/her? The *Norton Anthology of Poetry*. It's so big and glum-looking.

Who will play the poet in the Hollywood adaptation of your last poem? Naomi Watts.

What's your current favourite word? Squid.

You're proud of the poem but know it will offend someone you don't even like: what do you do? This is a good case in point. I'm not sure what Hugo Williams would make of 'Bird Belling', and I like him very much.

Would you rather win the TS Eliot Prize or the Prize Bonds? TS Eliot Prize.

Let's assume you're 60 and still publishing poems: what do you want to have achieved between now and then? I'd like to have written one or two poems that will make my children and my grandchildren proud.

Cyril Connolly said the true function of a writer is to write a masterpiece, and no other task is of any consequence. Do you agree? No. Trying to write a masterpiece is one thing. But then there's also trying to reach out. To remind us of what it is to be human, to be not afraid to bare yourself for the sake of the truth. And simply to entertain and delight.

'The hard part is getting to the top of page 1' – Tom Stoppard. What, for you, is the hard part? Remembering to keep a notebook on me at all times. And allowing myself time to write when there are so many other things I could be doing.

What advice would you give to older poets? Keep at it. I'm kidding. What could I possibly tell them that they don't already know?

Ciarán O'Rourke

KEEPSAKE

The stone
I cannot part with –

I anchor it daily
on the deep sea-bed
of pages by my desk,
a weight for paper
and for poems,
heartbeat-heavy,
but light enough
to let the summer whisper
in the sheaf
when windows open,
or when I leave,
thereby keeping
in its skull-dull, colourless,
life-perfecting way,
the rhythm
of this room adrift,

and your image, too,
pocketing sea-stones
years ago, your
white dress bright
on the eye-grey shore,
and you smiling there,
as if our wave's
unlovely sunder
would not come,
or as though the ocean
might remember touch,
the particles
be hurled again
as longing
from your fists…

Like here,
where words
must delve until

the element resists,
and the vivid
breath rebuild itself
from the little that persists.

LOVE SONG

The sun of sleep is rising in your head,
the colour of plum-love, and spoon-bright,
as the two moons that held me
close to crescents with a sigh, and sink.

The whisper softens to a breath.
In the pane above you, veils of web
window in mid-hum
the pendulum of a robin's hovering...

And if you were to waken now
under the far skies of this thought,
then you would know I made it for you,

that in the plum-dark wings of a robin
I heard a summer singing
and dreamed again of your limbs.

Ciarán O'Rourke

Were you a strange child with a taste for verse? Yes, in a way. Movies and books, stories and poems – there were plenty to go around in the house I grew up in. I once baffled a teacher in primary school by giving a plot summary of the Errol Flynn film *The Charge of the Light Brigade*, and then reciting an abbreviated version of Tennyson's poem as a coda. Odd reference points for an eight-year-old, but as the poet says, nothing goes to waste.

I probably began reading poetry 'full-time', so to speak, in my mid-teens. My first port of call was my parents' poetry shelves, which were (and remain) deliciously eclectic – I can remember first encountering *The Collected Poems of Richard Wilbur* there, which belonged to my Dad, and my Mum's *Selected Poems of Elizabeth Jennings*, and many more. I admit that I rarely understood what I came across on first reading. But poetry was accessible, at least in the sense that it was an available and relatively ordinary part of family life during my childhood.

Do you too dislike it? Only when it's not around, old toad that it is.

Who is your favourite character in a poem? Lately, Juturna from Virgil's *Aeneid* (Book XII).

If you could die and come back as a poem, what poem would it be? 'Birches' by Robert Frost. That would be good both going and coming back.

Someone offers you €1,000,000 to never write again: What is your response? Take the money, and write my benefactor a terrible ode.

Have you ever glued pages of a poetry book together? I'm sorry to say that I've never glued the pages of a poetry book together. I did once transcribe a poem onto a postcard, and sellotape it inside a hundred-year-old copy of Kant's *Critique of Pure Reason*. This done, I returned the book (unread) to the eminent library holdings from which I'd snatched it for the day. To my knowledge, the postcard was never discovered.

It's the centenary of the Easter Rising: does this fact matter to you and if so, in what way? For me the question of how to pay tribute to a revolutionary event like the Rising is a difficult one. Some would argue that no matter how exploratory the guiding principles may be, the process of commemoration naturally ends up as a sort of safety packaging for the incendiary gift-box that is the history itself. Exhibit the ash, but hide the flame. And if you've come for the rebellion, please queue on the left for the guided tour.

I sympathise with this viewpoint, and relish its pugnacity – while also confessing to a personal enjoyment of exhibitions and heritage sites. Perhaps I'll be the oddity who joins the next revolt, just so long as he's allowed to carry his placard in praise of keeping the museums (but out with admission charges!). Time will tell.

For now, it seems to me that developing a public discourse on the explosive beginnings of the State is a worthwhile project. However, this shouldn't serve just as a means of passing pious or pedantic judgement on old events. A valuable commemoration of the Rising will be one capable of addressing the lines of division, exclusion, and injustice that currently run deep in Irish society.

To my mind, the fate of the Rising cannot be decided by rationalising one mode of oppression over another kind of violence, or vice versa. If the State itself is the most formidable result of the Easter Rising, then the significance of that event takes on meaning only in light of our efforts to eradicate the glaring inequalities and subtle violences that persist in Ireland today. In this sense the Rising continues to ask the most vital questions of us. What principles currently govern our political life? What kind of society do we want to live in? What forms of commitment to that goal are possible now?

If someone described you as a political poet, what would your reaction be? Fishing for compliments is a dangerous business, especially when poems are concerned. But my basic attitude is as follows: whether the critical appetite is for sardonic sonnets or angry anthems, the reality is that this will have very little bearing on the writing of poetry, unless the author intuitively shares in that desire. If someone described me as a political poet, I'd be curious to know which party he voted for in the last election.

What's your worst poetry habit? As a reader, I have a reputation for not getting around to the books that my friends give or loan to me, which is inexcusable. When I'm writing, I often forget to eat, wash, and answer people when they talk to me, which is unhealthy. My worst poetry habit, however, is bad scansion: I couldn't tell a spondee from a spatula to save my life.

A family member says, 'You should write a poem about that': what do you do? Nod in agreement, while inwardly lamenting the fact that poems never do what I ask them to. If anything, the opposite is the case.

If your best poem were a weekend away, where would it be? Svalbard – which I imagine is cold, blue, and clear as a star. To write a poem like that might just be heaven on earth.

It's a good poem but it's forty-one lines long and the competition with the big prize specifies a max of forty: what do you do? I dislike changing poems after I've written them, especially when there's a competition involved. So in this instance, I would probably wallow in my penury, and try to persuade myself of the aesthetic merits of my forty-one line poem.

Who will play the poet in the Hollywood adaptation of your last poem? In the best of all worlds: Arthur Stanley Jefferson (aka Stan Laurel).

What's your current favourite word? Appetency, and just the way Ted Hughes says it when he reads Eliot's line in *Four Quartets*: '… while the world moves / In appetency, on its metalled ways / Of time past and time future'.

Cyril Connolly said the true function of a writer is to write a masterpiece, and no other task is of any consequence. Do you agree? I suspect that writers are basically useless creatures. An ignominious species that dedicates the best part of its time to scratching a cultural itch (of one form or another). They are the procrastinators of the word, and it's about time someone acknowledged the fact. How they produce a legible line, let alone a masterpiece, is beyond me.

What advice would you give to older poets? Maybe every poet is a young poet. Maybe all poets are born old already. Either way, my advice is to keep chasing the flame – because there's always the possibility that you or the young 'uns will need the light a little way down the road.

Michelle O'Sullivan

THE LUMBER ROOM

I.
Sapwood

Grey waters that say you must fall to your knees to enter.
It's rough, abstract molten glass –
though there's no feel to the wind at all.

Behind you a burr of hills, a feathered space edged between
blue and yellow; and this grist of light sharpening light,
the breadth of a grindstone.

You let your eye rest. And wait.
Cormorants dive and disappear.
Unseen hands are ripping silk.

II.
Heartwood

In the deepest part of the forest, you find the coldest
part of the floor – an un-waxed table, mute
asterisks of moss.

Hidden from stars, there's a faceless dark.
A dark like no dark before. Un-animal. Primal.
Somewhere a stag's foot has jutted against roots.

Night has offered to walk with you –
one side of its hand is gold, the other onyx.
You have refused the offer.

III.
Pithwood

How faithful grief is, returning to return
to remind you again, in the stillness
of near everything gone;

a picked-up slack tick of a blood-let
battered heart, muscle-flensed, oxygen-
desperate, willing itself to move on –

like the figure of a woman
who has just kissed the light
and is making her way indoors.

THE BLIND STEPCHILD

The note she said she didn't write is here.
And it says the impossible possibilities
have burned themselves to the quick:
like pressing my hand to the stove
and keeping it there.

Even when she said she couldn't say
what had been done,
the head's failures, the heart's triumphs
or vice versa: *it's all the same,*
a burthen of rotten wood that won't burn.

Her voice edging casual on the page, edging
pain – the thinned black words unbending
with their weight: *I keep pressing my hand*
to the stove, but it's cold.
And I can't burn.

Michelle O'Sullivan

Were you a strange child with a taste for verse? I can't remember not loving books, those big little worlds created by words. And I distinctly remember that feeling of wanting more, the excitement of what's next. So, yes. I probably was. (And still am).

Do you too dislike it? If the question is drawn down to the rawness and the raw material, the genuine – no. If it's the other palaver – yes.

Who is your favourite character in a poem? The 'I' in Keats's fragment 'This Living Hand'.

If you could die and come back as a poem, what poem would it be? 'The Panther', Rilke.

Someone offers you €1,000,000 to never write again: What is your response? Can I read the small print?

Have you ever glued pages of a poetry book together? No. (But I've turned the spine of a book to face the back-end of a bookcase. Just once or twice…)

It's the centenary of the Easter Rising: does this fact matter to you and if so, in what way? It does. No small thing, to challenge an empire. And to remember the remarkable men and women who did so is to recognise their legacy.

If someone described you as a political poet, what would your reaction be? I'd be intrigued about them as a reader.

Would you rather be the poet or the poem? I suppose that depends upon when the question is asked. Today, this given moment – I'd so rather be the poem.

If you could pick a time to be dropped amongst the three best poets alive at that moment, when would it be and who would they be? A fascinating time I imagine would be early Rome, and even more so – an evening with Sulpicia, Ovid and Tibullus.

What's your worst poetry habit? Self-criticism.

You've arranged a date for 8pm, but it's 8.10pm now. You're working on a poem and it's going well. What do you do? Good things come to those who wait.

Have you ever carried a poem by someone else around on your person? If so, what was it? Oddly, yes. (Does side pocket of my bag count?) 'The Pruned Tree' by Howard Moss.

A family member says, 'You should write a poem about that': what do you do? Mentally make a note never to write a poem about that.

If your best poem were a weekend away, where would it be? The Aeolian Islands.

It's a good poem but it's forty-one lines long and the competition with the big prize specifies a max of forty: what do you do? If I'm really into the competitions with the big prizes, what does that say about me?

Have you ever used a poem to seduce someone? If so, what poem was it? (And did it work?) I suppose this question depends on how we're using the word seduce. I imagine it's the conventional sense. In that case – no.

You're given a choice: either every poem or no poem you write from now on must use the word 'I'. Which do you choose? The latter.

Your friend is depressed: what's the very last poetry book you'd give him/her? It depends on the person and the severity of depression. Blind literary remedies can be a dangerous thing.

Who will play the poet in the Hollywood adaptation of your last poem? The Hollywood adaptation of my last poem… wouldn't it be something else, and not a poem?

You're invited to read in a major festival: what are your top three backstage demands? What if I'm not demanding?

What's your current favourite word? Skirk'd.

You're proud of the poem but know it will offend someone you don't even like: what do you do? If I'm worried about offending someone that I'm not that mad about – surely that requires further investigation. There's much to be said for integrity.

Would you rather win the TS Eliot Prize or the Prize Bonds? The former.

Let's assume you're 60 and still publishing poems: what do you want to have achieved between now and then? If wonder is the reinvention of humility, and if I have held on to that – I will have achieved something.

Cyril Connolly said the true function of a writer is to write a masterpiece, and no other task is of any consequence. Do you agree? I think there's something to be said for timelessness.

'The hard part is getting to the top of page 1' – Tom Stoppard. What, for you, is the hard part? Sometimes it's trust. Other times it's doubt.

If your ideal poem were an outfit, what would it look like? Something understated and beautiful at once.

What advice would you give to older poets? I don't know that I'm that precocious...

Is there any question you wish you'd been asked here (that you'd like to answer now?) Thirty questions is questions enough.

Breda Wall Ryan

TENDER LOVING CARE

The child meant for summer, they say, came early in April,
light as a poppy, breaths that were barely breaths
fluttered his day-lily lungs,
speedwell-veined eyelids shut to a future
of *TLC only* prescribed on his chart.

Rumours flew round our small town that the mother
shed never a tear, but her breasts wept
when his fingerbuds opened, boneless as blossoms.
She read the plea in his palm, fixed
a soft pillow for his head.

They say she came back once, after her sentence,
begged the baker to water his Easter-dyed chicks.
A pigeon racer at a loft near the graveyard
said someone the spit of her spat on a stone
and scrubbed off the moss.

There's talk here of pink-and-blue chicks sipping water
from a hubcap in a window of broken glass,
they say someone's seen an empty coop and a stranger,
and a flock of opal wings swooping over a grave.
Some say the devil exists; some say angels.

David O'Kane

The Acuity of Blindness V
Oil on canvas, 400 cm x 225 cm

W. www.davidokane.com

David O'Kane

The Acuity of Blindness II
Oil on canvas, 150 cm x 120 cm

W. www.davidokane.com

David O'Kane

The Acuity of Blindness IV
Oil on canvas, 50 cm x 40 cm

W. www.davidokane.com

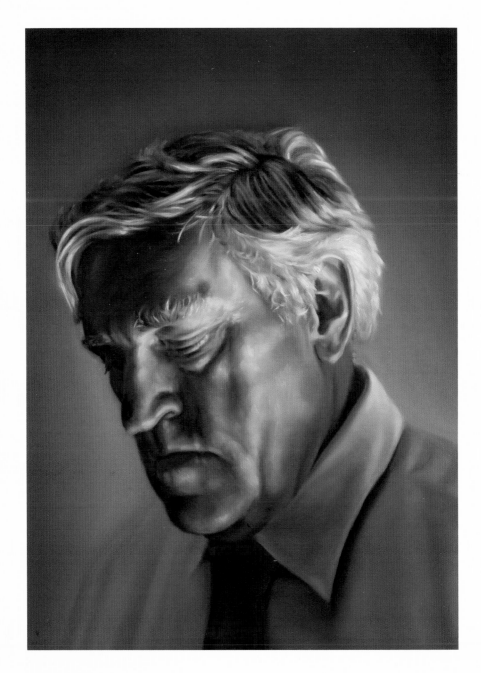

David O'Kane

The Acuity of Blindness VI
Oil on canvas, 70 cm x 50 cm

W. www.davidokane.com

Aoife Scott

Cistin Maggie, Mín an Leá
Etching and Aquatint, 70 cm x 50 cm

W. aoifescott1.wix.com/print

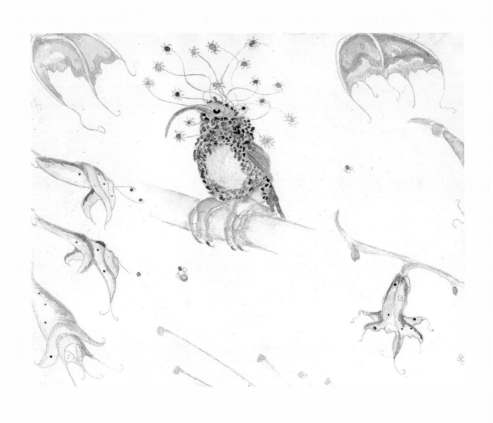

Melissa Ellis

Blue and Red Big Foot Bird
Intaglio Print with Watercolor, 19 cm x 25 cm

E. memelissaellis@yahoo.ie

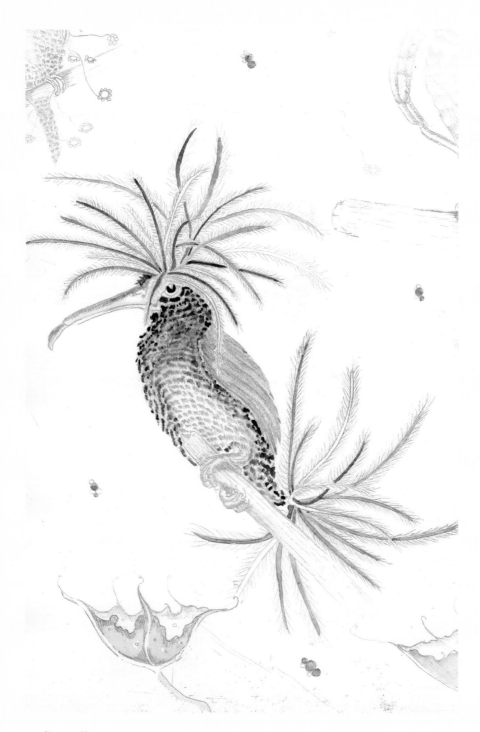

Melissa Ellis

Blue and Brown Mop Bird
Intaglio Print with Watercolor, 28 cm x 19 cm

E. memelissaellis@yahoo.ie

Aoife Scott

Solitude
Etching and Aquatint, 75 cm x 52 cm

W. aoifescott1.wix.com/print

Breda Wall Ryan

THE GATE CLANGS

in no wind and echoes,
echoes, and no one comes.
The harmonium groans,
the last congregant's gone.

A seal slick with oil spill
lies in my lap, pressing
his head under my chin.

Your pillow is dented
where no head will nestle again.
The single hair I save from the drain
I press in a book.

Dank air escapes the cellar,
the last of the turnips rots,
old newspapers yellow, unread.

It curdles the thin blade of my tongue.
I swallow. Swallow again.
Again it rises, curls my tongue's hem
around it. I taste it again.

I find it, new fledged, beak
agape and champing,
carry it home, build it
a nest in my belly,

feed it grey worms, taste
its fathomless hunger, know
it will never leave.

Breda Wall Ryan

Were you a strange child with a taste for verse? Verse inhabited the world inside my head. I preferred narrative poems to prose, I plodded along to slowed-down skipping rhymes and 'cured' grazed knees by chanting. Bawling calves, my mother's bow saw, a running stream; all spoke animal or metal or water which I heard as English rhyming couplets. A strange child? Isn't every child strange?

Do you too dislike it? I dislike, and love, the hours of word-wrestling, line-fretting, frustration.

If you could die and come back as a poem, what poem would it be? Any poem which, once heard, haunts your head and mutters under your breath – an 'ear worm' or 'garlic poem'.

Someone offers you €1,000,000 to never write again. What is your response? Writing is a compulsion. I'd take the cash, then go on writing in my head. Is that cheating?

Have you ever glued pages of a poetry book together? I've still got a Keats collection I glued with blood from a vicious paper-cut. Nobody borrows a blood-stained book.

It's the centenary of the Easter Rising: does this fact matter to you and if so, in what way? The hype around the 1916 centenary makes me angry and sad. Angry at the celebratory air around commemorative events; at the 'touristification' of a tragic time in our history. Sad at the lack of mourning for the civilians killed and injured and whose lives were ruptured. Sad that the Rising led to a long period of stifling repression.

If someone described you as a political poet, what would your reaction be? Labels such as 'political poet' are too constraining because they focus on a single aspect of a poet's work, ignoring the fact of artistic output being various. If a political poet is one who has designs on the reader, then I accept the label, provided the reader accepts that any designs on him or her came after the fact. I'm not a spontaneous poet; I need distance before I write a social protest poem.

Would you rather be the poet or the poem? The poet, ideally anonymous, so the poem would stand in its own light, free from the poet's shadow.

If you could pick a time to be dropped amongst the three best poets alive at that moment, when would it be and who would they be? I'd go forward a hundred years to discover where this evolutionary period in poetry will have led. Poetry is expanding through new technologies, multimedia, poetic experimentation and instant access to a readership via the internet, so I wouldn't stay too long in the future, in case I missed some momentous development in the present.

What is your worst poetry habit? I get absorbed in writing on the Dart and overshoot my stop by several stations.

Have you ever carried a poem by someone else around on your person? If so, what was it? I always carry a couple of collections and my notebook. When I'm lollygagging over coffee, I read. Or write – I love discovering something startling by misreading my handwriting.

A family member says, 'You should write a poem about that': what do you do? I say, 'It's your idea. You obviously feel strongly about it, so write it yourself.'

If your best poem were a weekend away, where would it be? In a cabin in a sun-dappled clearing surrounded by deep forest. Solitude.

It's a good poem but it's forty-one lines long and the competition with the big prize specifies a max. of forty: what do you do? Edit. Again. But I wouldn't mutilate it.

Have you ever used a poem to seduce someone? If so what poem was it? (And did it work?) Once, early in a relationship, I was given Dylan Thomas' *Complete Poems*. I was instantly smitten, by poems and giver. So seduction by poem works; I just haven't tried it myself.

You're given a choice: either every poem or no poem you write from now on must use the word 'I'. Which do you choose? Since the 'I' in a poem is an assumed persona, I'd avoid 'I', then find ways to bend the rule.

Your friend is depressed: what's the very last poetry book you'd give him/her? I'm unqualified to prescribe for such a serious illness.

You're invited to read in a major festival: what are your top three backstage demands? I want fair pay and conditions. Show me the money, give me a meal voucher and, if you value your electronics, a spill-proof water bottle.

What's your current favourite word? Gumption. Frazzle. Whiffle. That's three.

You're proud of the poem but know it will offend someone you don't even like: what do you do? Publish. Find the poem's readers. Offence is preferable to no reaction.

Would you rather win the TS Eliot Prize or the Prize Bonds? The Prize Bonds is like gambling, isn't it? I'd prefer the TS Eliot, because it's earned. Luck plays a part, but it's mostly hours and hours of work.

Cyril Connolly said that the true function of a writer is to write a masterpiece, and no other task is of any consequence. Do you agree? The function of a writer is to write. 'Masterpiece' may not be within her reach, but reaching is its own reward and 'good enough' is good enough.

'The hard part is getting to the top of page 1' – Tom Stoppard. What, for you, is the hard part? It's all hard, and all rewarding.

If your ideal poem were an outfit, what would it look like? A photographer's camouflage or a beekeeper's hat and veil. It would obscure the poet while allowing the reader to see the world of the poem from the poet's perspective. Does that make sense?

What advice would you give to older poets? I wouldn't dream of offering advice to experienced poets. My advice to myself is, 'Don't repeat, just because something has been successful. Risk. Dare. Be part of the change.'

Is there any question you wish you'd been asked here (that you'd like to answer now?) Yes: why do you go on, even when you can't? Because poetry is inevitable.

Declan Ryan

A VALLEY OF APPLAUSE

Is this where we would have had to go?
We might have made it here –
the other side of a bridge
from everyone we loved,
our plans, the shape we'd made
in the universe's lack.

Just off a train,
the rails curling round
and out of sight
we could, your hand in mine,
have stood a state of willed amnesia –
the sky a pyre – shaken off our shame
like dogs who'd swum through oil.

Frontier life,
water and shelter life,
imagine our first night:
unstoried earth to walk on,
a river to wash our hands
and mouths with,
hills to stop our gods from staring in.

The only words we'd need
would be 'I'm safe'
or 'start again',
your scent a lotus flower,
my skin broken by your teeth
like soft applause.

Remember you said
we should admit the way we felt
however difficult?
I'm saying now,
too late for you to waste your life.
Here isn't where we would have gone

but where I always was:
cut off from sun,

green-shadowed on all sides by noble boundaries.
The sky is hellfire.
I burn like coal,
whose heart is unforgetful coal.

AND I SAW THE LORD, WHO WAS A KINGFISHER...

And I saw the Lord, who was a kingfisher,
beside me among the cricket-songs of June.
I cannot understand that bird as one who suffered,
its bones too light for hanging.
I am furthest from it when I need a god who died
and think, then, it is my cousin that they killed,
who as a boy branded himself with boiling water,
stole cars and broke his mother's ornaments.
Having left with strength still about him
I could see him hauled up in that fashion
before a crowd who would not choose to spare him,
those he'd wronged cheering his decline.
If ever we met he was a fright or inconvenience
but I knew him capable of childish kindness
so I would have his death serve some purpose,
repairing what I've done that now needs mending,
so the world might once again be summarised
into two cheese rolls, a mirror-ball of foil,
a girl kneeling to brush green from her dress
and that bright Prince of air to dignify us.

Declan Ryan

Were you a strange child with a taste for verse? Strange I'm sure yes but I didn't have much to do with verse for a long time; it was always more Subbuteo, then when I was of an age, music. Verse came later.

Do you too dislike it? Yes I'm afraid I largely do, with certain unavoidable fondnesses.

Who is your favourite character in a poem? I like Weldon Kees's Robinson at the minute but no one else really springs to mind, maybe someone from a Les Murray poem, they often seem like good sorts.

Someone offers you €1,000,000 to never write again: What is your response? How thoroughly will they be policing this? I would like the money enormously.

It's the centenary of the Easter Rising: does this fact matter to you and if so, in what way? In a loose way I suppose it does, in that sort of back of the mind place where one might think about things like history and nationality, being already the ex-iest of ex-pats. I've lived in London my whole life, almost, so there's a certain residual pride in the whole thing but from a distance of many stripes. As a callow youth I was drawn to that idea of the sacrificial element in the way I was taught about it, the grand gesture. I like grand gestures, even (or perhaps especially) futile ones.

If someone described you as a political poet, what would your reaction be? It depends on their tone of voice really. I think it's a fraught notion, I would hate to be sloganeering, or to have designs, but I think there are political decisions that go into almost any poem, however well promoted those decisions become in the final thing. I admire a poem like Kavanagh's 'Epic', say, or the War poems of Keith Douglas and Alun Lewis. Things that can touch on the big themes but keep them personal and closely observed and don't go off with bombast or loudspeakers. I don't like the school assembly voice.

Would you rather be the poet or the poem? I'm a Lowell fan so I don't know if I could separate them. One life and all that.

If you could pick a time to be dropped amongst the three best poets alive at that moment, when would it be and who would they be? To be around at a time when Lowell, Berryman and Bishop were publishing would be quite something.

You've arranged a date for 8pm, but it's 8.10pm now. You're working on a poem and it's going well. What do you do? I would probably keep working, but I would at least make up a reasonable lie. There may be exceptions made, that said.

Have you ever carried a poem by someone else around on your person? If so, what was it? All the time yes, like a little relic or something. Too many to name, Hugo Williams often appears though, in the linings of jackets.

A family member says, 'You should write a poem about that': what do you do? Scowl meaningfully, although when this has happened it's usually as a joke.

It's a good poem but it's forty-one lines long and the competition with the big prize specifies a max of forty: what do you do? I've found that I tend not to fare well in poem competitions so I don't ever enter them now. I'd always try to let the poem be as long as it seemed to want to be though. I don't want to sound all hippyish about it, but I think if something's been written cynically for a purpose like that it tends not to be a very good thing all round.

You're given a choice: either every poem or no poem you write from now on must use the word 'I'. Which do you choose? Every, they probably will anyway…

Your friend is depressed: what's the very last poetry book you'd give him/her? I probably wouldn't inflict poetry on them at a time like that, but the last would be some apparently cheery optimistic thing, about the triumph of the spirit and such like. No one needs a skein of geese at a time like that.

You're invited to read in a major festival: what are your top three backstage demands? I've never wanted to write Nina Simone's request for 'champagne, cocaine and sausages' more in my life, but realistically if I was allowed to sit down unmolested indoors I would already feel blessed enough.

You're proud of the poem but know it will offend someone you don't even like: what do you do? I think I'd almost always go ahead with a poem that I liked if I thought it worked and wasn't gratuitously offensive, with the usual caveats of not being a total arsehole. And to go back to the political idea, there's a sort of implicit offense in most poems anyway, if you're talking about people you don't like in a stylistic sense. The sort of poems I write are probably aesthetically quite offensive to certain poets, and vice versa, I think it's generally better not to worry too much about 'offense'. I'd rather be honest than palatable.

Let's assume you're 60 and still publishing poems: what do you want to have achieved between now and then? I'd like to have written at least a couple of books that I'm proud of, even if they're not the sort of thing I'm still doing. It's difficult to say really, it's on a poem-to-poem basis I'm generally working. To have written at least five or six poems that I still think are good would be a win.

What advice would you give to older poets? Something I've often thought about is the idea of how you develop as a writer, and I'd always be interested in seeing a poet reflect where they are now rather than falling back into being a caricatured version of themselves, or of their greatest hits, over and over. I'm much more interested in the late Rick-Rubin-produced Johnny Cash album where his voice cracks and he's frail than one where he was still pretending to be a gunslinger, and the same is true in poems. There's nothing that gets the cringe-reflex working harder than men of a certain age pretending to be dangerous Byronic seducers when the only heart that's fluttering is their own, and that due to a serious medical unpleasantness.

Stephen Sexton

ANNIVERSARY

The giddy cathedral swooned –
the night had been unremarkable for being remarkable
and was much like 1916 and mostly unlike the Titanic.
It would have been her twenty-fifth birthday, he said
of the older sister he always felt had been his shadow
who appeared in dreams as a porch light in the mist,
an igloo once, once as the breast plate and harness
of Dolph Lundgren as He-Man. The bars were closing.
Young men sallied in the streets like riderless horses.
She never had a name, he said, so he thought of one.

The avenue he lived on then reeled around a gigantic
horse chestnut tree and the pavement was lousy
with conkers and seedcases. He said, you know
everything in the world either is or isn't that tree.
Standing at the wrought iron railings we recognised
a man we'd never seen before.
His distressed leather doctor's bag was handsome
and he opened it.

Stephen Sexton

A TALENT

Of two minds where to go for dinner
we darkened the door of the fortune teller.
The table draped with satin was set for three.
I thought of the unfinished game of draughts
we waltzed through heroically that afternoon
and longed not to know how it would end.
Candles burned on shelves, dust conspired
among the curios: a horse's foot, a rabbit's shoe.
She took our hands and read them simultaneously
and from them somehow divined what I was thinking:
who tells the fortune of the fortune teller?

A sadness entered the room and introduced itself.
I propped a little mirror in front of her.
She made not head nor tail of her reflection
so we asked the fortune teller out to dinner.
A man will come and he will hold a mirror
was all she cared to say.
I thought of a green summer and the garden
I grew up in, and as someone said, how
nostalgia might best be remedied by pain
and terror.

Stephen Sexton

Were you a strange child with a taste for verse? I wrote a poem at school when I was eight or so. It was two quatrains about a mayfly and was probably a great insight into what I felt about death at the time. My teacher, though, questioned one of my rhymes. The word that troubled her was 'nowt', as in naught, or nothing. I think I picked it up from *Coronation Street*. I knew it sat weirdly in my vocabulary, but the rhyme must have demanded it, whatever that was. It wasn't pretty. I think I changed it.

If you could die and come back as a poem, what poem would it be? 'From March 1979' by Tomas Tranströmer. The poem seems to contain so many moods, chief among them, perhaps, is a suspicion of the efficacy of language and, by extension, itself as a poem.

Someone offers you €1,000,000 to never write again: What is your response? I'd like to say yes, but I'm not sure what I'd occupy my time with. Someone said there's no money in poetry. This offer would seem to suggest there's money in no poetry, which is the last place I'd think to look.

Have you ever glued pages of a poetry book together? Do people do that? Is it the equivalent of skipping a bad track on a pretty good album?

It's the centenary of the Easter Rising: does this fact matter to you and if so, in what way? I'm interested in how we're obliged to respond to the 'decade of centenaries'. Of course, I care more about what's remembered than how it's remembered, to whatever extent they're separable. The space there is between commemoration and celebration was made the most complex for me when the Frames Complex (a pool and snooker hall in Belfast) chose, in 2012 or thereabouts, to change the name of its restaurant from 'Frames' to 'The Titanic Pub and Kitchen' to take advantage of the anniversary. Then there's the SSE Arena's 'Titanic Burger', which is a burger 'topped with barbecue sauce and a selection of onion rings', an obvious reference, we understand, to the life rings thrown from the sinking ship into the North Atlantic.

If someone described you as a political poet, what would your reaction be? I'd want to make the distinction between political poetry and a political poet and what the latter is expected to do. Were I a political poet, I expect I'd have written about the lack of reproductive rights in Ireland, and what seems like contempt for marriage equality from some parties in the north, but it's obvious these positions need to change; I don't feel the need to reiterate what seems obvious in a poem. I'm disinclined to think a poem has any real utility.

Would you rather be the poet or the poem? 'O body swayed to music, O Jeroboam, / How can we know the poet from the poem?'

The implication is, I guess, that 'the poem' is finished and complete and incapable of deviating from itself. On the other hand, 'the poet' gets to write another one, a better one perhaps. The poet has, it seems, more possibilities to do other things, or even quit all together. I think I'd rather be the poet, but it's a tough call because I don't even like dancing.

A family member says, 'You should write a poem about that': what do you do? Since no one in my family – that I know of – writes poems, I'm genuinely interested to know what they think poetry does or should do. Often, someone has figured one thing resembles another, or that something is at odds with another thing. And I agree, there's something about Vince McMahon (former professional wrestler and CEO of WWE, b.1945), and his huge arms, in the ring with men at least half his age. He takes falls softer than he used to, he sells feints less convincingly than he used to. He gets himself up again, though, with those huge arms.

You're given a choice: either every poem or no poem you write from now on must use the word 'I'. Which do you choose? Every poem would use the word 'I' where the 'I' can accommodate many voices and positions. On the other hand, Douglas Hofstadter has it that 'the "I" is a hallucination hallucinated by a hallucination'.

Who will play the poet in the Hollywood adaptation of your last poem? This reminds me of my idea for a TV talent show where contestants compete to write poetry that is assessed and commented on by a panel of 'experts'. A languid voice-over would say things like 'Maria hasn't heeded Judge Andrew's advice about the comma in line four – let's see how he reacts.' Judge Andrew explodes, naturally. Judge Lorraine says something about form and content and Maria is sent home. Peter performs a double villanelle in the final and wins. Peter always wins. Anyway, Paul Rudd.

You're invited to read in a major festival: what are your top three backstage demands? Bottled water, Dylan's Live 1966 Royal Albert Hall Concert and something to play it on. I would like to have my wits about me should anyone at the poetry festival call me 'Judas'. The WiFi password.

What's your current favourite word? Roustabout.

Cyril Connolly said the true function of a writer is to write a masterpiece, and no other task is of any consequence. Do you agree? I can't imagine setting out to write a masterpiece is a good idea. You want the next poem to be better than the last and the one after the next to be better again. Actually, you want all of them to be so good that people not only take their hats off to you, they burn their hats and pledge to go bare-headed in your honour, but we can't all get what we want.

'The hard part is getting to the top of page 1' – Tom Stoppard. What, for you, is the hard part? The hardest part for me is knowing when to start. I tend to let ideas marinate for a bit and see what other things get attached to them. It's the legacy of no ideas but in things, I think. However, if I let things marinate for too long, they spoil, or I lose the thread, so to speak. Not missing the window is the hard part.

If your ideal poem were an outfit, what would it look like? When I read, let's say, a formal poem, or a poem that is crafty (which is to say it displays 'craft', whatever that is), or at least a poem with end rhymes, a fixed metre, witty line breaks et cetera, I find myself aware of how wimpy or slight, by comparison, the start of each line is. This makes me think of one of those novelty aprons with a tuxedo on the front worn by someone who is otherwise naked. An ideal poem would, for me, resemble elegant casual wear worn by a celebrity with a dark secret.

Michael Naghten Shanks

LOVE / HOTEL / LOVE

To escape the foreign city we found ourselves
in the darkened foyer of the *heart heart heart*

hotel, hovering over the automated check-in screen,
inputting credit card details, our illuminated faces

debating how long we wanted to spend together.
We were buying this moment of comfort, ready-made

for translation into memory. Pink and blue neon lights
lined the skirting of the narrow hallway that led to our room.

Inside, a ceiling mirror created doppelgängers
who looked down on us in tired bewilderment.

The submarine-esque room was dimly-lit, windowless;
warm furnishings the only thing that stopped us

feeling claustrophobic. We lay on the bed,
talking to each other through our mirrored selves.

Michael Naghten Shanks

SOME QUESTIONS

Why am I awake? Does anyone want to design a website for me? Any ketamine? Why was I born a poet? Where should I submit my essay on insomnia? Who's coming to Cork with me tomorrow? Can I put 'Tweets about Bears for online literary journal' on my CV? Which Bear outfit should I wear tomorrow? Exactly what did I instigate? How? Why are you so angry? A 60-line triptych poem about an imaginary Hollywood starlet: who publishes those? Why am I awake? Does my body not remember what I did to it last night? Any jobs? Is it really complicated or do you just like to make things complicated? Do you ever walk around the supermarket holding a bunch of broccoli like it's a bridal bouquet? Does anyone else think we've jumped the shark w/r/t septum piercings? Should I ask her out for Valentine's Day? When will we ever get the ophiocordyceps unilateralis themed Lars von Trier remake of *Antz* or *A Bug's Life*? Am I right in thinking it would've been weird to ask this random guy on the bus where he got his awesome jumper? What do you suppose the hairspray budget is for Sky Sports News? Should I just be really fucking egotistical and compose a cento out of lines from my own previously published poems? Have I been speaking French without realising it? Having a salad for dinner makes up for having jaffa cakes for breakfast, right? It's mojito season, right? Can we all agree that February will be the month we go out, drink whiskey, and dance to Beyoncé? Does anyone else have an urge to lunge wildly at the Pope?

Michael Naghten Shanks

Someone offers you €1,000,000 to never write again: What is your response? I accept the offer and use the money to fund a new creative pursuit. Poetry exists outside of words.

It's the centenary of the Easter Rising: does this fact matter to you and if so, in what way? No.

If someone described you as a political poet, what would your reaction be? I'd brace myself for their satirical poem that would no doubt follow soon after.

Would you rather be the poet or the poem? The poem, because it never has to take responsibility for the failings of the poet.

What's your worst poetry habit? Imagining an ideal reader.

You've arranged a date for 8pm, but it's 8.10pm now. You're working on a poem and it's going well. What do you do? Stop writing – there's enough mental masturbation in the world of poetry – and apologise to my date for being late.

If your best poem were a weekend away, where would it be? London.

It's a good poem but it's forty-one lines long and the competition with the big prize specifies a max of forty: what do you do? Forget the competition and wonder what I could do to make it a great poem.

Have you ever used a poem to seduce someone? If so, what poem was it? (And did it work?) Yes.

You're given a choice: either every poem or no poem you write from now on must use the word 'I'. Which do you choose? No poem must use 'I'. The subjective experience of the poet is always present in the poem.

Who will play the poet in the Hollywood adaptation of your last poem? Shia LaBeouf.

Let's assume you're 60 and still publishing poems: what do you want to have achieved between now and then? A closer understanding of what I'm trying to say and an acceptance that I'll never be able to say it.

'The hard part is getting to the top of page 1' – Tom Stoppard. What, for you, is the hard part? Accepting the misreadings of the reader.

What advice would you give to older poets? Read younger poets as contemporaries.

Is there any question you wish you'd been asked here (that you'd like to answer now?) Do you think it's possible for there to be an annual 'Best Irish Poets' series? Yes, but the choice of editors each year would be crucial.

Róisín Tierney

CHAUCER

When I think of Sylvia Plath
declaiming Chaucer to the cows,
how they crowded round her, rapt,
their blue-black eyes reflecting sky and field
and her pale figure straddling a gate,

I think of my sister and me, children
rattling along on the bumpy tractor-cart,
being followed across a field by eager kine;
her growing terror at their growing boldness,
her flash of tears.

A bullock herd in full bucking gallop –
a fearful sight to a tremulous child.
Looming in they slowed to a gentle amble,
starry foreheads pressing in around us,
great dark eyes rolled up toward the sky.

The tractor cut its din, and halted.
Its great roar gone, we heard only
the soft moans of the beasts and birdsong.
Our damp girl-breath, ribboning the air,
mixed up with calf-breath, sickly, sweet.

School-skirted, we crouched, raised our hands,
stroked the massive skulls, pressed down rough curls.
We let them lick our knees – they like the salt.
Then we sang to them *The Foggy Dew*,
Star of the Sea… They flicked their ears.

Emboldened, we recited everything we knew,
The Flattered Flying Fish, and the one about the sage
who wondered much and sorrowed more
because it hung behind him…..
Our cart a stage, the bullocks in our thrall,

we wrung our small fists, died violently and slow,
recovered, staggered to our feet, began again.
(Oh, we littered the firmament with tears,

fainting for want of pity, potatoes, bread!)
Our pied audience semi-circled us and stared,

dipped their stippled lashes, peered some more,
transfixed by our strange show. A full half-hour
we held them, till we were all played out,
the engine roared, and they shot off,
kicking and giddy into the rain, the glister
of *Aprille shoures* under the *yonge sonne*.

PITCHBLENDE

How could Maria Skłodowska, as she was then known
when she first stepped from the Flying University

onto the streets of Paris, have guessed,
that her findings would one day set her lab aglow,

electrify the air, thin her blood fatally
as she lined her pockets with them:

radium, polonium? (This last named after her country).
How could she ever have guessed

that the burn from these would be so rare
that they would not only cauterise

my mother-in-law's bladder, my father's throat,
but so douse her manuscripts, her precious notes

that they would have to lie softly
at the heart of the great *Bibliothèque Nationale*

in a lead lined-chamber,
for a half-life of approximately

one-thousand-six-hundred years?

Róisín Tierney

Were you a strange child with a taste for verse? Perhaps. I was mad about
books and dogs – or any animal really. Reading-wise, I took in anything
and everything: adult stuff, children's stuff, the backs of cereal packets,
whatever. I read walking home from school, under the desk at school,
and under the blankets in bed. Mostly prose, though someone gave me a
children's poetry anthology which had poems like 'The Traveller', 'The
Fish' and 'The Highwayman', and wonderful drawings. I really liked it
when we read poems aloud at school too.

Who is your favourite character in a poem? Bess, the landlord's black-eyed
daughter (in 'The Highwayman'), for her heroism; the Wife of Bath for
her earthiness; the farmer's bride, in Charlotte Mew's beautiful poem, for
staying true to her instinctive nature.

If you could die and come back as a poem, what poem would it be? 'The Second
Coming'? Only joking… 'The Silken Tent', by Robert Frost.

Someone offers you €1,000,000 to never write again: What is your response?
If they could pay it in instalments, a hundred thou a year, and I didn't
have to toe the line until the final instalment was paid, I would definitely
consider it.

*It's the centenary of the Easter Rising: does this fact matter to you and if so,
in what way?* Yes, I grew up in Dublin and was aware of our history and
the long political struggle for independence. My great-grandfather was
Eoin MacNeill. After the rising he was in gaol in Kilmainham, and then
Dartmoor and Lewes in the UK. After his release he was a member of
the first Dáil and Minister for Education. My grandmother often talked
about him, and that period of history, to us. She showed us his prison hat,
which she still had. It really was white with black arrows on it!

If someone described you as a political poet, what would your reaction be?
I would think they had misunderstood me. I am not a political poet,
though I do hold political opinions. I am quite socialist in my outlook,
but I do not write socialist poems. Some people can write political poetry
and get away with it, but too often it can feel, to the reader or audience,
as if you are being lectured to, told what to think. Brecht is often guilty
of that. Yeats managed an exception, in 'Easter 1916'. But I think he was
writing about a really changed state, rather than telling people how to
think.

If you could pick a time to be dropped amongst the three best poets alive at that moment, when would it be and who would they be? I would like to have met Keats. And John Clare. Is two good enough? Or in a different era the writer of 'Lament for Art O'Leary', Eibhlín Dubh Ní Chonaill, because it is such a beautiful poem, and because we know so little of the early women poets. As Virginia Woolf said: 'Anon, who wrote so many poems without signing them, was often a woman.'

Have you ever carried a poem by someone else around on your person? If so, what was it? Yes, more than once. 'The Death of the Hired Man' by Robert Frost. 'Ode on Melancholy' by Keats. Bishop's 'The Fish'. At the moment, 'Snow' by Louis MacNeice.

If your best poem were a weekend away, where would it be? Do you like that poem 'In Paris With You' by James Fenton? I do. Or that other poem, in Irish, by Tadhg Ó Dúshláine, 'Leathchéad i bPáras'… Paris is very romantic. But I think for me it might have to be Granada, Lorca's home, where I lived for a while. That's a poetic city definitely!

Have you ever used a poem to seduce someone? If so, what poem was it? (And did it work?) I have not set out to, but poems *are* seductive, a way of communicating intimately and making readers drop their guard.

You're given a choice: either every poem or no poem you write from now on must use the word 'I'. Which do you choose? It would definitely be no poem. I actually adopted this as a device, for about a year when I first started writing seriously. Because my earlier poems were stymied by too much 'I'. Adopting the tactic forced me to write from many different stances and viewpoints, and I think was greatly helpful.

Your friend is depressed: what's the very last poetry book you'd give him/her? Upbeat, jolly stuff is really the worst thing to give someone at those times. Like being forced to listen to Christmas muzak when your head is hanging off. So I would steer them away from the anthology of funny poems, or anything with an uplifting or inspirational promise in the title… Plath would probably be okay. When I was very depressed, I was comforted by listening and re-listening to *Krapp's Last Tape*.

You're invited to read in a major festival: what are your top three backstage demands? A decent mike. Twiglets. Free booze.

What's your current favourite word? It varies, though I will always love the word *heifer*. It is beautiful on the page, beautiful to say, and to hear, and it brings a beautiful image to mind: a young, speckled cow with semi-crescent horns, turning her head around over her back to stare. It has got heft and grace at the same time.

I also love many very ordinary words – for example *water* and *air* – I think for their elemental resonance, and their 'r' endings, which can either be enhanced (Ireland) or disappear (England), depending on your accent.

And I like some onomatopoeic words too. The *scutters* – as in a dose of the runs. Repeat four or five times quite quickly, and you'll get the idea: *scutter, scutter, scutter, pharp! scut…* Beautiful!

But as your question intimates it changes all the time. At the moment I am slightly in love with the word *this*. Because it rhymes with *kiss*. Because it adds empha*sis*.

Let's assume you're 60 and still publishing poems: what do you want to have achieved between now and then? I am probably closer to 60 than some of the other poets answering this questionnaire! Another few collections. Perhaps, among them, four or five really great poems?

Cyril Connolly said the true function of a writer is to write a masterpiece, and no other task is of any consequence. Do you agree? I think you are always aiming for a masterpiece. And I think, even of our best writers, out of a whole life's work, you can expect only about five truly sublime poems. So that is what you are aiming for. But it doesn't mean that no other task is of any consequence. When I think of MacNeice I always think first and foremost of 'Snow'. But that doesn't mean that I don't get a great deal of pleasure out of his other poems.

If your ideal poem were an outfit, what would it look like? I am not sure, but it would not look anything like a cape.

Jessica Traynor

BERRY

My grandmother looked down
on women who called them *berries* –
threw strained upward glances
as we scoured the shops for one
the day my granddad died.

A funeral without a hat?!
In her mind all ninety years of her
still wrapped
in that slender body
from the photo on Howth head;

a spill of curls falling
from the beret she wore
at just the right angle,
that made the hat
speak volumes,

suggesting, as it did,
one raised eyebrow.
And in the orange light
of the haberdasher,
she pronounced the word

as if holding a single snowflake
in her mouth: 'A ber*et*,
do you have a ber*et*,'
while the shopkeeper rifled
through a sale-item basket,

until, miraculously, it appeared:
fledgling-soft to perch
on her white hair
like some dark protecting bird –
'there's your berry.'

On that day, she allowed
the slip to go unmentioned
as we fussed about her,
and the berry took its place –
a new object in her catalogue of grief.

Jessica Traynor

SYMMETRY

You move the shed, electrics and all,
to one side of the garden

and back again. We argue, then relent.
Hildegard von Bingen had visions

of such perfect symmetry,
shapes and colours, snowflake-infinite,

and you see that possibility here;
for each petal on each flower

to find its match across
the perfect-circle lawn.

But there are obstacles:
the bloody shed

headache-inducingly singular,
preventing your moulding

of the natural into the ordered.
Hildegard would commiserate,

and we do too – we know
what this mania means –

that you're seeing shapes and colours
in the corners of your eyes,

fractured auras, night-terrors –
before long, another seizure.

We watch you from the kitchen,
know how to let this take its course,

to patch you up once symmetry
has released its grip.

Jessica Traynor

Were you a strange child with a taste for verse? I was. My Granny was a Speech
and Drama teacher and so rhymes have been floating around my head
from a very young age, things like 'Antigonish' by Hughes Mearns, which
is a deeply sinister piece of verse and attracted and frightened me in equal
measure. I still think this is the effect poetry should have on the reader.

Do you too dislike it? I read an article by Ben Lerner in the *London Review
of Books* recently where he talks about this Marianne Moore poem,
and about the various reasons to dislike poetry. He proposes that even
seemingly technically perfect poems are exercises in failure; it's that old
chestnut about the imperfection of language and its inability to adequately
channel experience. I'm sympathetic to this point of view I think, but I
do believe that our bockety and broken communication systems afford
us glimpses of perfection, or the illusion of perfection – and that another
approach to the argument might be that perfection, by its very nature, is
something that can only ever be glimpsed, and maybe poetry offers those
glimpses?

Someone offers you €1,000,000 to never write again: What is your response?
To read the small print for loopholes – does dictation count? What about
pseudonyms? If I could break the rules and get away with it, I would
definitely take the money…

*It's the centenary of the Easter Rising: does this fact matter to you and if so,
in what way?* I suppose my initial reaction is to acknowledge the anxiety
across the country about the right way to commemorate one moment
in history. How to encapsulate the meaning of the Rising for the generations alive today? I was bewildered by the notion of the Defence Forces
presenting a tricolour and a copy of the Proclamation to every school,
especially since the Proclamation is effectively irrelevant in the wake of
the 1937 Constitution. Here's a blueprint for how it could have been! The
accompanying notion of asking each child to write their own version of
the constitution seems much more inspiring. I am deeply concerned with
the importance of history, but not as something that should be viewed
in a bubble, and without interrogation of its connection to the present
moment. I heard Gabriel Gbadamosi speak recently on the dangers of
becoming too absorbed in the past. One quote in particular stuck with
me: 'If you legislate for the dead, the future belongs to the dead'. And so
surely anything we give to our children now, in commemoration of the
Rising, should be useful for their present and their future while acknowledging the past.

Ultimately, I feel any connection to the life or ideas of those who fought in the Rising was broken long before I was born. The divided but diverse Dublin of the pre-Rising years is only alive on the pages of *Ulysses*. The intervening generations wiped it out, and we look at it now across an unreachable gap. It may as well have happened in another country. All of this sounds very negative, I suppose, but mightn't it be liberating too?

If someone described you as a political poet, what would your reaction be? I would thank them. I'm interested in what is meant by 'political poetry'. Working in theatre, there's often a sense that work isn't political unless it's dealing directly in political ideology or debate or diatribe. This reminds me of the negative reaction of many nationalists to the première of Synge's *Playboy of the Western World*, as discussed in Roy Foster's *Vivid Faces* – not only did it not depict a kind of native Irish life that suited their Victorian morality, it wasn't 'political' enough; it didn't strike a note for freedom. But now we would consider this play, I think, as a strongly political statement on the nature of Irish life at the time. I'm less interested in political poetry as a blunt statement that preaches to the converted and cosily reinforces ideas they already hold. Rather I think of it as having a troubling or disturbing potential; the proper aim of any poem.

What's your worst poetry habit? Knottiness. The thought or idea tripping up the rhythm of the poem.

You've arranged a date for 8pm, but it's 8.10pm now. You're working on a poem and it's going well. What do you do? I would keep working on the poem and show up late to give the false impression that I'm a fun and spontaneous kind of person.

It's a good poem but it's forty-one lines long and the competition with the big prize specifies a max of forty: what do you do? I would find a way to make it forty. One of the processes I enjoy in poetry is the opportunity to use those lateral thinking skills which don't come naturally to me. I've always enjoyed the challenge of form, and found it a good means of interrogating the work itself.

You're given a choice: either every poem or no poem you write from now on must use the word 'I'. Which do you choose? I find the notion of dispensing with the 'I' really intriguing and it's a challenge I might set myself at some point. However, I don't think we should underestimate the dramatic potential of 'I'. I listened recently to some of Ted Hughes's BBC recordings on poetry, where he talks about writing about family and that interesting mixture of personal experience and imagination that allows any writer to create. Hughes is writing about his brother, but it's a brother that bears no resemblance to his actual brother. 'I' gives the writer this licence, and expands to encompass anything the poet can imagine. Many first person poems have little to do with the writer's own experience, and are all the more interesting for this.

Let's assume you're 60 and still publishing poems: what do you want to have achieved between now and then? A small audience of people who, on hearing I've a new book coming out, think 'Oh, I'll look forward to that.'

What advice would you give to older poets? I remember interviewing my grandmother, born in 1916, when she was in her nineties, and being surprised by her unwillingness to tell me much about her life. She was clinging to the secrets of people long dead. And I realised my own naivety, in asking her to talk about her life in the open way I would talk about my own. So the advice I would give is the advice I had no right to give her – but it's advice I would certainly give myself. Don't keep your secrets. We live in a country smothered by generations of silence. Talk about the grey areas of your experience. I also think we have a tendency to only salvage 'good' or 'bad' narratives from history, and anything more complex is rarely spoken about. The best poetry challenges or disturbs. Disturb us.

Eoghan Walls

PEAR STONES

Skinning the baby's pear with my teeth
I dislodge a lump from its grainy flesh
like a singular gravel beneath the peel,
a warped nut of pear fibres coalesced
from itself, just like tissue may harden
in the ripening of a milk-heavy breast
but drier – more like the knots of skin
on the cuticles on the hand of a carcass
ossifying in the hermetitude of a coffin
but as I am footering, the big wet mass
is clawed out of my fingers to her lips
as she descends on the fruit, ravenous,
first gnawing a pulp from its sugary tip,
working into the stump and the seeds
the juices and stone, the fibres and pith.

Eoghan Walls

BUOYANCY

Rutting bull seals might take pity on me here, caught
mid-coitus in the eyes of my upright child in her cot,

as I'm ballasted from the darks of sub-glacial space
breathless to these bright holes gnawed in the surface.

My blood decompresses too quickly as I near the air
and a world creaking with the footfall of arctic bears.

The stare of the child can barely reflect on anything,
say the seals. Foraging must happen. Turn and sink,

and they're right, but there's more moving in her eyes
than there are shadows treading over the polar ice.

Eoghan Walls

Were you a strange child with a taste for verse? I was a gobby child. I wanted
to be Houdini first. I got them to tie me up and put me head down into a
bin – I asked for it – and would try to escape. After that, I wanted to write
ghost stories. Poetry came later.

Do you too dislike it? Yes. But it is the closest thing to real magic I know.

Who is your favourite character in a poem? The body.

If you could die and come back as a poem, what poem would it be? 'Jabber-
wocky'.

*It's the centenary of the Easter Rising: does this fact matter to you and if so,
in what way?* Hmm. Not at all. I got angry during the recession. I was
earning very little from part-time short-term contracts; like everyone
else we were angry at being taxed aggressively to bail out private business. Everyone I talked to – everyone – was constantly bitter, and yet in
2012, when the public endorsed the government's push for austerity, I
kind of gave up. We had to leave Ireland – one family of many financial
emigrants – looking for work elsewhere. When the only party with any
strong left-wing aspirations is Sinn Féin – and they are constantly rejected
in the Republic for their associations with the Dirty North – then I think
we have more pressing problems of political consciousness than a group
hug for collective green-Jingoism, and will be suspicious of whose
interests the celebrations will serve.

If someone described you as a political poet, what would your reaction be? I
would be happy – if I could manage to combine my political desires with
my aesthetic requirements. But all poetry is political anyway – particularly when it focuses on 'unpolitical' material, like childbirth or sex or
domestic moments. Turning from the jazz and vajazzle of the public
eye to something fresh and intimate is a political act. The celebration of
lanugo, or a brief exchange with a migrant on the Dart, or a supremely
well-fried egg, is a political act. Perhaps this looks like a kind of apathy.
But it is our job to expand the world for the reader or listener; we can
only do this through avoiding the familiar outrage of public discourse.

What's your worst poetry habit? Possibly writing in the voice of a pigeon.

*You've arranged a date for 8pm, but it's 8.10pm now. You're working on a poem
and it's going well. What do you do?* Pause and wonder how I got into this

strange world. Check I still have children. Ask the wife if she minds me going out on a date. Duck promptly. Ask her if she knows where the kids are.

A family member says, 'You should write a poem about that': what do you do? I pull a face and say 'Dead on, no bother.'

It's a good poem but it's forty-one lines long and the competition with the big prize specifies a max of forty: what do you do? Jiggle the line endings.

Have you ever used a poem to seduce someone? If so, what poem was it? (And did it work?) Yes; it was a twee but cute kid's poem about a mouse, a catapult, the moon and a smashed piano to nab the tears of my then-future-wife. She, for her part, had made me a hammock. I think it was a fair swap.

You're given a choice: either every poem or no poem you write from now on must use the word 'I'. Which do you choose? It would be easier to lose the 'I' than to keep it; I am halfway to its execution already.

Your friend is depressed: what's the very last poetry book you'd give him/her? Christopher Reid's *A Scattering* – a marvellous book – particularly for bereavement.

You're proud of the poem but know it will offend someone you don't even like: what do you do? Publish it at the first opportunity.

Let's assume you're 60 and still publishing poems: what do you want to have achieved between now and then? To have written a few more good books. And steered the rest of my life between the rocks. Some massive poems – not in length, but in scope – big world-changers – that would be good.

Cyril Connolly said the true function of a writer is to write a masterpiece, and no other task is of any consequence. Do you agree? Jeepers. Do writers have functions? Like a spanner or a dishwasher? I think what we have to do is make the world bigger for the reader – for the moment of the poem – and hopefully long afterwards – we have to expand the horizons of the world through direct sensory engagement – in a tight machine of language. But saying it like that is dangerously dogmatic. Part of what I want from writers – what I want – is that they are on the move; tricky to define, a kind of renegade, adapting their work to society around them. If we offer social critique, it should be in the form of ideological terrorism. Not just the power to shock the reader, but also something gentler, like the difference between shock and surprise. Yes – that one great poem is a high ideal, and possibly helpful when you are in the fits of rewrites and word-choices; but after that, you have to write the next poem.

What advice would you give to older poets? Which older poets? If you mean our poetic forbearers, I would offer them more thanks than advice. If there is a hegemony of stuffy old farts – the subtext to the question, it seems – those farts have been as keen to experiment and expand the art as us yoof – am I the yoof? – and it was the old guard that laid the groundwork that got me into poetry. If you put a gun to my head, I could say something about making room for more new voices in poetry – but I do not think it is the poets themselves who are the agents of whatever exclusions there are in poetry. Oh – here's something; sometimes you read too quietly at readings. Speak up a bit.

Adam White

ALL GOLD CREEK, 1901

Any old man here going over life
is listened to, though no one could hold
       our attention once. We had to cross
       an ocean. We had to trudge
a thousand miles of nightmare ice for gold.

In the cabins stories always start with this:
the cruel pick-and-shovel going down in the hole
       of each claim; how much piling up pay-dirt
       pays out in Dawson in the end;
how some lose the head there and flutter whole

pokes of the stuff, until, as sure as the veins
of the Klondike are filthy rich in ore,
       late-night crosstalk
       and the old songs
sift rough nuggets of our folklore

from the mud of this entire venture.
The Salmon of Knowledge or Fionn mac Cumhaill,
       a telling of Tír-na-nÓg
       by big Bucket Ass Clancy
I sat beside in school

who, turning in, always says 'We were rich
then too, but didn't know it,' like the lad
       recalling how his mother used to say
       the grass is somehow greener,
the shop fare sweeter than when you've had

it, from an already disappointing elsewhere.
When you think of it a life might
       abound in secrets, but the point
       can't be some race to crack them: just missing
a thing's enough to know you did it right.

Adam White

THE FALLS FURTHER ON

We always live our lives upriver
from them, so that here the quiet course
of water seems to sit sheet metal-still.

Sky and leaves are on it like a patina.

But the day there isn't any wind
cresting the trees, or needful thrust
in the day, you do hear something

of that distant roaring overpour

where every minute the ass falls
out of the whole damn thing,
plummets and reloads

into the pure ongoing rest of itself.

Adam White

Were you a strange child with a taste for verse? I would say *estranged* more
than strange. I recall having little interest in the classes at school, often
being only physically present, passing the time by scribbling out song lyrics
from memory in my copybooks, then repeatedly reading them back to
myself. I sometimes think about the fact that none of them made any
sense. Take for instance 'Doll steak, test meat … Angel left wing, right
wing, broken wing. Lack of iron and/or sleeping. Protector of the kennel.
Ecto-plasma, Ecto-Skeletal', which is from a Nirvana song I can still recite
from memory. I just loved the sound and the unmistakable rhythm of it.
Consequently, when I started writing my own lyrics, which didn't make
any sense to me either, my main aim was just to make them a pleasure to
sing/say out loud. So that was where I got the initial taste for verse, and I
see now that it was good training for the ear.

Who is your favourite character in a poem? The grandfather in 'Manners', by
Elizabeth Bishop. He's a lovely old man, kind to both people and animals,
and seems very wise and tolerant. He's certainly one example of how
we should live our lives. When I see people in a café, or a pub, staring
at the screens of their phones and not acknowledging each other at all, I
often think of his advice to 'remember to always / speak to everyone you
meet'.

If you could die and come back as a poem, what poem would it be? 'The Trees'
by Philip Larkin: 'Last year is dead, they seem to say, / Begin afresh,
afresh, afresh.' They're good lines to have in mind when you have to
start anything anew. It's almost impossible to choose one poem, really,
but having to, I'd choose that one, in lieu of coming back as an actual
tree.

Would you rather be the poet or the poem? The poet, perhaps, because in the
end the poem isn't really anything other than a poem, while every poet is
so much more than a poet.

*If you could pick a time to be dropped amongst the three best poets alive at that
moment, when would it be and who would they be?* The late Seventies, I think,
when you had Heaney and Hughes meeting in Heaney's house for drinks
and poetry and songs. Then Philip Larkin could drop in and we'd all go
fishing in the morning.

What's your worst poetry habit? Reading poems on long boring drives. I
mean while driving the car. I do it less now, due to an incident where
reading a really good Heaney one nearly killed me.

You've arranged a date for 8pm, but it's 8.10pm now. You're working on a poem and it's going well. What do you do? Jot down any remaining ideas and leave quickly. In my experience, anything that's going well usually benefits from a short break. Then, of course, if the date goes well you might get a poem out of it!

Have you ever carried a poem by someone else around on your person? If so, what was it? Yes, once. It was a poem called 'The Peace of Wild Things', by Wendell Berry. I copied it out on a piece of paper and carried it to read at my uncle's funeral. One of the undertakers really liked the poem, so I passed it on to him. I like to think that he might have shared it with someone else.

If your best poem were a weekend away, where would it be? I'm already 'away', so it would actually be a couple of days at home: short, sharp and mostly memorable.

You're given a choice: either every poem or no poem you write from now on must use the word 'I'. Which do you choose? Easy: no more poems with the word 'I' in them. The best poems tend to incorporate some story, and you don't need to use the word 'I' to tell a good story.

Your friend is depressed: what's the very last poetry book you'd give him/her? Something by Philip Larkin, surely. *The Whitsun Weddings*, say. I know there's a lot of wit in there, and they're all delightful poems, but imagine giving stuff about life being a deception, a disappointment and 'slow dying' to someone suffering from depression!

You're invited to read at a major festival: what are your top three backstage demands? 1. A quiet place to think before reading. 2. A generous drop of 15-year-old Redbreast to think with. 3. A free dinner afterwards with the other readers.

What's your current favourite word? I learned the French word *assortiment* recently, and I thought it was a beautiful word, so I suppose that qualifies. The fact that I had never heard it made me think of how little most of us manage to enhance the type of language we use from day to day. It's a pity, because we use and reuse a pretty limited bank of words, when you think about it, when getting tired of using the same words distorts communication. There are so many lovely ones out there that are a pleasure to say and hear out loud that could help us feel we're closer to what we're actually trying to say and save us from the disappointment of being misunderstood.

Cyril Connolly said the true function of a writer is to write a masterpiece, and no other task is of any consequence. Do you agree? I could agree with the first part of that, in a way, but not the second. When you're writing new material, especially when you're putting together a new book, you sometimes stop and ask yourself the question, *Why am I doing this? I mean, what's the point?* And if you don't feel that what is new is somehow different than, or an improvement on, what came before, it's hard to see the sense in it after a while. Therefore you're always looking for some kind of evolution in your writing. So why not say that your true function is to write a masterpiece, in that it should be about constantly, gradually, developing your writing, and striving for this, seeing and believing that you're working towards *your* 'masterpiece'?

'The hard part is getting to the top of page 1' – Tom Stoppard. What, for you, is the hard part? Right now, the hard part is getting to the top of the stairs (where my desk is)! Nothing to do with frailness: it's more freeness, or free time that's nowhere to be found. We're always busy here, mostly with preparing for the day job (teaching), so any brainwork like poetry has to be put on the back burner. The last time I made it to that quiet place to write was during the summer holidays. But then, mightn't that be part of what Stoppard meant?

Adam Wyeth

OAK

The old oak is our father
coming home late at night,
turning his key in the door,
leaving it off the latch.

The leaves are still falling.
I hear his slippered footsteps
shuffle on the stairs, scuff
along boards. He stifles

a cough opening my door
and releases the catch
from the window, taking
my breath as the curtains

mushroom. A pattern
of webbed branches frames
the moon. His great shadow
bows low and creaks

down the years, pressing his
whiskered cheeks to my brow,
whispering *good night*.
The old oak swishes and moans,

low mutterings meander
through the house. The wind
brushes my face, the sound
of leaves falling, patting the pane.

The moon is in the wind
and the wind is in the bough
and the bough is in the door
that our father leaves open.

Adam Wyeth

METAMORPHOSIS

The words are turning in on themselves
and then turning into something else.
They are turning over and under like birds
dipping in water, turning the reflection
of trees into rings and ripples in the lake.
They are asleep and then they wake
in the whiteness of the page. Black-licked
words fall like leaves littering the reflection
of the day, then are released birds.

Adam Wyeth

Were you a strange child with a taste for verse? Poetry played no great part in my life until I was a teenager and left secondary school. When I was sixteen a poem poured out of me that was pure catharsis and probably pure doggerel, but there was some latent power in it that I found hypnotizing. An old friend then gave me Shakespeare and Walt Whitman's complete works. I was never the same again. When I was very young though I used to write down the lyrics of songs from my mum's record collection. Then I did the same with hip-hop when that came out. I attempted writing one or two raps myself. I guess that was really my start into creative writing, though I didn't know it then.

Do you too dislike it? I love literature of all kinds, just as I deeply love all kinds of music – from Rachmaninoff to Radiohead. Duke Ellington said something like there are only two types of music: good music and bad music. That might sound glib but there's a lot of truth in it. The established poetry world can be a pretty stuffy place though, at times, that jostles and froths with snobbery, elitism and egomania. What was it Auden said? – 'No poet or novelist wishes he were the only one who ever lived, but most of them wish they were the only one alive, and quite a number fondly believe their wish has been granted.' The academia surrounding poetry can still be a formidable fortress that often produces a type of poetry that is perfectly formed and perfectly dead. As a reaction to this, performance poetry has been on the rise, bringing the spoken word back to the people, but this has also brought its own kind of inverted snobbery, narcissism and ignorance. Most performance poetry is ranting tabloid sensationalism and lacks the more subtle layers of metaphor and craft. Marianne Moore's poem, to which your question refers, is a good reminder that no artist can afford to rest on their laurels... or their Hardy!

Who is your favourite character in a poem? Eliot's 'Prufrock' is pretty irresistible.

If you could die and come back as a poem, what poem would it be? Whitman's 'Song of Myself'.

Someone offers you €1,000,000 to never write again: What is your response? I'm wondering if I could dictate my poems and still take the money.

Have you ever glued pages of a poetry book together? Only my own. I made a pamphlet of *Silent Music* a few years before Salmon took it in 2011. That strange child with a taste for verse, Derek Mahon, launched it for me in Kinsale, which was a real honour and delight!

It's the centenary of the Easter Rising: does this fact matter to you and if so, in what way? The Celtic Revival from this period fascinates me. Ireland's poets and its ancient myths played a key part in informing and forging its identity today. It's easy to be dismissive of the Celtic Twilight now and to be unaware of the impact Celtic culture has made on Ireland, Europe and much of the world, not to mention the influence it has had on its writers. It's no accident that three of the most important and influential figures of world literature, Yeats, Joyce and Beckett came out of this period. Even though Joyce jokingly called it the 'cultic toilette', his work is deeply embedded in mythology, as the punning title of his last great work shows, *Finnegans Wake*: 'Finn again is awake'.

If someone described you as a political poet, what would your reaction be? I'd probably think they haven't read my work. Saying that, Pinter was writing political plays from the start before he knew it. His plays though are ultimately metaphors and metaphors are always doing more than one thing.

Would you rather be the poet or the poem? The poem. I think it was Paul Durcan who said he is trying to disappear in his work, or words to that effect. The author should never stand in front of a poem or get in the way of what it's trying to do or say.

If you could pick a time to be dropped amongst the three best poets alive at that moment, when would it be and who would they be? The Romantic or Elizabethan period is for me the most tantalising … I'd love to meet Shakespeare, Burbage and the gang, not to mention get to the bottom of what really happened in that tavern brawl with Kit Marlowe.

What's your worst poetry habit? Perhaps having a tendency to tie up the end of poem a bit too neatly.

Have you ever carried a poem by someone else around on your person? If so, what was it? Robin Flower's sonnet, 'Say not that beauty is an idle thing'.

If your best poem were a weekend away, where would it be? Barcelona or the West of Ireland.

Have you ever used a poem to seduce someone? If so, what poem was it? (And did it work?) I wrote my partner romantic love poetry while we were courting. I'm not sure if it seduced her but she gave a lot of useful suggestions. She's still my best critic.

You're given a choice: either every poem or no poem you write from now on must use the word 'I'. Which do you choose? I'd probably go without the 'I' as it would be more of a challenge.

Your friend is depressed: what's the very last poetry book you'd give him/her? I think all good poetry, no matter how dark, is a boon to the reader. Often the darkest stuff is the most exhilarating and humanizing – take 'The Ballad of Reading Gaol'.

Who will play the poet in the Hollywood adaptation of your last poem? James Franco seems to play all the poets at the moment, so he can do it. Otherwise Cate Blanchett; if she played Bob Dylan she can do anything.

What's your current favourite word? Numinous.

You're proud of the poem but know it will offend someone you don't even like: what do you do? Publish and be damned!

Let's assume you're 60 and still publishing poems: what do you want to have achieved between now and then? Writing is a very personal and instinctive thing for me. I'm in my work so it's very hard to talk of it beyond that. I hope I can look back though and say I have been true to the work and to my imagination and hope that some of it has a life of its own.

Cyril Connolly said the true function of a writer is to write a masterpiece, and no other task is of any consequence. Do you agree? Absolutely, you've got to aim for the stars… but I prefer Beckett's take, 'Try again. Fail again. Fail better.' When you give yourself permission to fail and write rubbish you allow the subconscious to take over and that's often when the magic begins.

'The hard part is getting to the top of page 1' – Tom Stoppard. What, for you, is the hard part? For me, the real work happens after the first draft. I often equate my writing process to throwing all my toys out of the cot and then afterwards trying to assemble them into some semblance of order.

If your ideal poem were an outfit, what would it look like? A cream-white silk blouse and tight navy-blue pencil skirt with the sound of French stockings swishing underneath.

What advice would you give to older poets? Do poets grow up?

Notes on Contributors

Graham Allen is Professor in English in UCC. He was the winner of the 2010 Listowel Single Poem Prize and has been shortlisted for various other awards, including the Shine / Strong Award 2015. His e-poem *Holes* and his collection *The One That Got Away* (2014) are published by New Binary Press. A new collection, *The Madhouse System*, is due for publication this summer.

Tara Bergin is from Dublin. Her first collection, *This is Yarrow*, was published by Carcanet Press in 2013, and was awarded the Seamus Heaney Centre for Poetry Prize, and the Shine / Strong Award for best first collection by an Irish author. She currently lives in the North of England.

Dylan Brennan's poetry, essays and memoirs have been published in a wide range of international journals. Currently based in Mexico City, he is the author of *Atoll* (Smithereens Press, 2014), *Blood Oranges* (The Dreadful Press, 2014) and co-editor of *Rethinking Juan Rulfo's Creative World: Prose, Photography, Film* (Legenda Books, 2016).

Sarah Clancy is an award-winning page and performance poet from Galway. Her first collection *Stacey and the Mechanical Bull* was published in 2011 by Lapwing Publications, and she has published two further collections: *Thanks for Nothing, Hippies* (2012) and *The Truth and Other Stories* (2014), both with Salmon Poetry.

Jane Clarke's first collection, *The River* (2015), is published by Bloodaxe Books. Originally from Roscommon, she now lives in Wicklow. Her work is widely published and her awards include the Listowel Writers' Week Poetry Collection Prize (2014), and the Trócaire / Poetry Ireland Competition (2014).

Adam Crothers was born in Belfast in 1984. He lives in Cambridge, working as a library assistant, literary critic and teacher, and as a Commissioning Editor for the online magazine *The Literateur*. A contributor to *New Poetries VI* (Carcanet Press, 2015), he is the author of *Several Deer* (Carcanet Press, 2016).

Paula Cunningham lives in Belfast. Her books, both from Smith | Doorstop Books, are the pamphlet *A Dog Called Chance* (1999), and *Heimlich's Manoeuvre* (2013), which was shortlisted for the Fenton Aldeburgh, Seamus Heaney Centre, and Shine / Strong first collection prizes.

Ailbhe Darcy's first collection, *Imaginary Menagerie*, was published by Bloodaxe Books in 2011. More recent poems have appeared in *gorse, Poetry,* and *The Stinging Fly.* This summer she will perform her work in Cyprus as part of the European Omnibus tour organised by CROWD.

Martin Dyar's debut collection, *Maiden Names* (Arlen House, 2013), was a book of the year selection in *The Guardian* and *The Irish Times,* and was shortlisted for both the Pigott Poetry Prize and the Shine / Strong Award. He was the winner of the Patrick Kavanagh Award in 2009.

Elaine Gaston is from Ireland's north coast. Her first poetry collection *The Lie of the Land* (Doire Press) was published in 2015. She was longlisted for the inaugural Oxford Brookes International Poetry Prize and received a Commendation in the Vincent Buckley Poetry Prize, 2015. She was educated at Oxford University and at Queen's University, Belfast. She received an ACES award from the Arts Council of Northern Ireland in 2015 and currently lectures at Ulster University.

Eleanor Hooker's second poetry collection, *A Tug of Blue,* is forthcoming from Dedalus Press. Recently, she was awarded First Prize in *Bare Fiction*'s Flash Fiction competition. She is Programme Curator for the Dromineer Literary Festival, and helm and Press Officer for Lough Derg RNLI Lifeboat.

Caoilinn Hughes is currently Visiting Writer at Maastricht University in the Netherlands. Her debut *Gathering Evidence* (Carcanet Press, 2014) won the Patrick Kavanagh Award and the Shine / Strong Award (2015). Her poems have appeared in *Poetry, Best British Poetry, Best New Zealand Poems, PN Review* and elsewhere. An extract from her novel-in-progress has been published in *Tin House* (Spring 2016).

Andrew Jamison is from Co Down. His first collection, *Happy Hour,* was published by The Gallery Press in 2012. He teaches English at Bristol Grammar School.

Victoria Kennefick's debut poetry pamphlet, *White Whale* (Southword Editions, 2015), won the Munster Literature Centre's Fool for Poetry Chapbook Competition (2014) and the Saboteur Award for Best Poetry Pamphlet (2015). A winner of the Red Line Book Festival Poetry Competition, her work has appeared in *Poetry,* New Irish Writing in *The Irish Times,* and *The Stinging Fly.*

Marcus Mac Conghail: ☺ = ✏ + ♪

Robert Herbert McClean is an experimental writer and audio-visual artist. His work has appeared in *The White Review, gorse,* and *The Irish Times*. His artist statement can be viewed online (**robertherbertmcclean. info**), and his debut collection, *Pangs!* (2015), is available from Test Centre (**testcentre.org.uk**).

Afric McGlinchey is a Hennessy Award-winning poet whose debut poetry collection, *The Lucky Star of Hidden Things* (Salmon Poetry, 2012), was translated into Italian and published by L'Arcolaio. Her second collection, *Ghost of the Fisher Cat* (Salmon Poetry, 2016), has been nominated for the Forward Prize for Best Collection (**www.africmcglinchey.com**).

Jim Maguire's first collection of poems, *Music Field* (Poetry Salzburg, 2013), was shortlisted for the Shine/Strong Award in 2014. A past winner of the Strokestown Poetry Prize, he works as an adult education teacher in Wexford, where he lives with his family.

Christodoulos Makris' books are *Spitting Out the Mother Tongue* (Wurm Press, 2011) and *The Architecture of Chance* (Wurm Press, 2015) – chosen as a poetry book of the year by RTÉ Arena and *3:AM Magazine*. He has curated numerous projects and events, including the transnational poetry collaborations tour *Yes But Are We Enemies* (2014), which involved more than 40 contemporary poets from Ireland and Britain. He is the poetry editor of *gorse*.

Geraldine Mitchell was born in Dublin and lives on the Co Mayo coast. She won the Patrick Kavanagh Award in 2008 and has since published two collections, *World Without Maps* (Arlen House, 2011) and *Of Birds and Bones* (Arlen House, 2014).

Julie Morrissy is a poet from Dublin living in her home city after spending a number of years in North America. In 2015 Morrissy was shortlisted for the Melita Hume Poetry Prize and selected for the Poetry Ireland Introductions Series. Her debut pamphlet *I Am Where* (2015) is available from Eyewear Publishing.

Emma Must is a student in the Seamus Heaney Centre at Queen's University Belfast. She was awarded second place in the 2013 Strokestown International Poetry Prize, and the Templar Portfolio Award in 2014. Her debut pamphlet *Notes on the Use of the Austrian Scythe* was published by Templar Poetry in 2015.

Doireann Ní Ghríofa writes both in Irish and in English. She was awarded the 2015 Ireland Chair of Poetry bursary by Paula Meehan. Her books include *Résheoid* (2011) and *Dúlasair* (2012), both published by Coiscéim, and *Clasp* (Dedalus Press, 2015), shortlisted for the 2016 *Irish Times* Poetry Now Award.

Mary Noonan's poems have appeared in *The Poetry Review, PN Review, The Dark Horse, Poetry London, The Spectator* and *The Threepenny Review*. Her first collection – *The Fado House* (Dedalus Press, 2012) – was shortlisted for the Seamus Heaney Centre Prize and the Shine / Strong Award. In 2014, she was awarded an Arts Council of Ireland Literature Bursary.

Rebecca O'Connor's debut collection *We'll Sing Blackbird* (Moth Editions, 2012) was shortlisted for the Shine / Strong Award in 2013. She is the recipient of a Geoffrey Dearmer Award, and her poems have appeared in *The Forward Book of Poetry, The Guardian, The Spectator* and *The Stinging Fly*. She is co-director of *The Moth*.

Ciarán O'Rourke was born in 1991, and lives in Dublin. His poems have appeared in a number of publications in Britain and Ireland. He was winner of the Cúirt New Writing Prize 2009, and his pocket-pamphlet *Some Poems* was published as a Moth Edition in 2011.

Michelle O'Sullivan's *The Flower and the Frozen Sea* (The Gallery Press) was published in October 2015 and is a Poetry Book Society Recommendation.

Declan Ryan was born in Mayo and lives in London. He is poetry editor at *Ambit*. A pamphlet of his poems was published in the Faber New Poets imprint in 2014. He works at King's College, London, where he edits **wildcourt.co.uk**.

Stephen Sexton lives in Belfast where he is studying for a PhD in Creative Writing at the Seamus Heaney Centre for Poetry. His poems have appeared in *Poetry London* and *Best British Poetry 2015*. His pamphlet *Oils*, published by The Emma Press in 2014, was the Poetry Book Society's Winter Pamphlet Choice in 2015.

Michael Naghten Shanks is editor of *The Bohemyth*. He has featured in various publications, including *gorse*, *3:AM Magazine*, and *The Best New British And Irish Poets 2016*. In 2015 he was shortlisted for the Melita Hume Poetry Prize and selected for the Poetry Ireland Introductions Series. His debut poetry pamphlet, *Year of the Ingénue* (2015), is available from Eyewear Publishing.

Róisín Tierney taught for several years in Spain (Valladolid and Granada), and now lives in London. She read in Dublin as part of the Poetry Ireland Introduction Series in 2008. Her pamphlet *Dream Endings* (Rack Press, 2011) won the 2012 Michael Marks Award. Her collection *The Spanish-Italian Border* (2014) is published by Arc Publications.

Jessica Traynor's first collection, *Liffey Swim* (Dedalus Press, 2014), was shortlisted for the 2015 Shine / Strong Award. She was awarded the 2014 Ireland Chair of Poetry bursary and is currently under commission by the Ireland 2016 centenary programme. Poems have appeared in *Poetry Ireland Review, Hallelujah for 50ft Women* (Bloodaxe Books, 2015), *One, The Penny Dreadful, The Stony Thursday Book,* and *If Ever You Go* (Dedalus Press, 2014).

Breda Wall Ryan's fiction and poetry have been widely published, broadcast and anthologised. Poetry awards include the iYeats, Poets Meet Painters, Dromineer Literary Festival, Over the Edge New Writer of the Year prizes (2013), and the Gregory O'Donoghue International Poetry Prize (2015). Her first collection, *In a Hare's Eye* (Doire Press, 2015), won this year's Shine / Strong Award.

Eoghan Walls lectures in Creative Writing at Lancaster University. He has received an Eric Gregory Award and an Irish Arts Council bursary, while his first collection, *The Salt Harvest* (Seren Books, 2011), was shortlisted for the Shine / Strong Award.

Adam White is from Youghal in east Cork. His years training and working as a carpenter in Ireland and France were the main inspiration for his first collection of poetry, *Accurate Measurements* (Doire Press), which was shortlisted for a Forward Prize in 2013. A second collection will be published this year, also by Doire Press.

Adam Wyeth is a poet, playwright and essayist, living in Dublin. His debut collection, *Silent Music* (Salmon Poetry, 2011) was Highly Commended by the Forward Poetry Prize. His second book, *The Hidden World of Poetry: Unravelling Celtic Mythology in Contemporary Irish Poetry* (Salmon Poetry) was published in 2013. Wyeth's third collection *The Art of Dying* is forthcoming from Salmon Poetry. He teaches creative writing online at **www.fishpublishing.com** and **www.adamwyeth.com**.